Jessica Joelle Alexander is a bestselling author, parenting expert and cultural researcher. Her work has been featured in the *Wall Street Journal*, BBC World News, the *New York Times*, CNN and many more. *The Danish Way of Parenting*, which Jessica co-authored, has been published in thirty-three countries. She's been a spokesperson for LEGO on the power of play, and gives talks on parenting, education and happiness around the world. She speaks four languages and lives with her husband and two children in Copenhagen. See more at jessicajoellealexander.com and thedanishway.com

Camilla Semlov Andersson is a Danish family therapist and author with over twenty-five years' experience working with parents, families, schools and kindergartens all over Denmark. She has published three books and has a private practice outside Copenhagen. See more at parogfamilieterapeut.dk and heledeleborn.dk

Praise for *The Danish Way Every Day*

'It is one thing to commit yourself to a positive, respectful, uplifting, trustful mode of parenting. It is quite another to carry it out, every day – or as close as you can to every day – through the inevitable ups and downs of daily life. Jessica and Camilla provide a wonderful, practical tour through essentially all the situations with kids, from 0 to 16, veering towards *hygge*. I wish this book had been available when I first became a parent. I recommend it to every parent, and to grandparents, too!'

Peter Gray, Research Professor of Psychology and Neuroscience and author of *Free to Learn*

'This book translates "the Danish way of parenting" into action! It provides great insights and guides the reader through many concrete aspects of day-to-day parenting of children at different ages. I know it will be my future go-to manual, offering a wealth of hands-on advice and inspiration. After reading this book I feel motivated and excited to try out some of the many fun and *hyggelige* ideas on how to connect more with my children and turn "me-time" into "we-time"!'

Line West, cross-cultural parent and anthropologist

T0385287

'As a psychologist and now parent educator for 25 years, I have found myself in thousands of discussions with parents about key concepts that are so important to understand for the well-being of children. And, without a doubt, in almost every single one of those discussions, the question "but what do I DO?!" comes up. *The Danish Way Every Day* is perhaps the most brilliant capture ever written of bringing to life the day-to-day rhythm of what it is that our children actually need to thrive. Developmentally informed and heart-centred, this book is a wonderfully structured guide for how to help your children (and you!) live exactly as nature intended. I will be recommending it to all.'

Dr Vanessa Lapointe, author, speaker, parent-champion

'*The Danish Way Every Day* offers a treasure trove of insights to help parents maintain meaningful connections with their children throughout babyhood to adolescence. The book's thoughtful exploration of relationship-nurturing practices and ways to create *hygge* in daily life provides a refreshing alternative to the anxiety-driven approaches so common today. This beautiful guide is filled with actionable ideas that any parent can implement immediately. For those seeking to foster closeness while raising resilient, confident children, *The Danish Way Every Day* is an essential addition to your parenting library.'

Greer Kirshenbaum PhD, author of *The Nurture Revolution*

'*The Danish Way Every Day* is easy to digest and easy to use. It helped me immediately communicate better with my tween and teen, speaking to them with logic and love, and allowing us to all feel better about the new dynamics we found ourselves working within. The practical layout of the book made it a daily dip-in, dip-out lifesaver that reminded me to stay calm, be kind and not worry about the small stuff when it comes to raising healthy, happy children.'

Sarah Ivens PhD, bestselling author of *Forest Therapy*

The Danish Way Every Day

Jessica Joelle Alexander

with

Camilla Semlov Andersson

PIATKUS

PIATKUS

First published in Great Britain in 2025 by Piatkus

1 3 5 7 9 10 8 6 4 2

A CIP catalogue record for this book
is available from the British Library.

ISBN: 978-0-349-44015-6

Typeset in Baskerville by M Rules
Illustrations on pages 105 and 140 by David Andrassy
Printed and bound in Great Britain by Clays Ltd, Elcograf S.p.A.

Papers used by Piatkus are from well-managed forests
and other responsible sources.

Piatkus
An imprint of
Little, Brown Book Group
Carmelite House
50 Victoria Embankment
London EC4Y 0DZ

The authorised representative
in the EEA is
Hachette Ireland
8 Castlecourt Centre
Dublin 15, D15 XTP3, Ireland
(email: info@hbgi.ie)

An Hachette UK Company
www.hachette.co.uk

www.littlebrown.co.uk

Acknowledgements

Jessica

Thank you ...

Sophia and Sebastian, my greatest teachers and the lights of my life.

Søren – so many mountains we have climbed together. Here's to many more.

Mom and dad, for *being* the Joneses, and the best parents in the world.

Camilla – for your wonderful contribution to this book.

My dear friends and sister. My village. You know who you are.

And to Denmark – for making me a better person every day. I am humbled to share your wisdom with the world.

Camilla

Thank you ...

Nicky – for believing in me. I couldn't have done this without you.

Our three children, who inspire me and teach me so much.

My former colleagues and dear friends. Our deep talks make me a better mom.

And Jessica, for helping me see the Danish Way. It is so clear to me now.

Contents

Introduction

'Do not ask your children to strive for extraordinary lives.
Such striving may seem admirable, but it is the way of foolish-
ness. Help them instead to find the wonder and the marvel of
an ordinary life. Show them the joy of tasting tomatoes, apples
and pears. Show them how to cry when pets and people die.
Show them the infinite pleasure in the touch of a hand. And
make the ordinary come alive for them. The extraordinary
will take care of itself.'

William Martin, *The Parent's Tao Te Ching:*
Ancient Advice for Modern Parents

The Danish way of parenting

Before I had children, I wasn't considered the most maternal
person in the world. I wasn't even sure I wanted to have children. When I met my Danish husband, and went to Denmark
for the first time, however, my life completely changed. The
children all seemed so serene, content, respectful and well
behaved. There was almost no yelling and parents looked
genuinely joyful. The simplicity of childhood was valued
and treasured in a way I had never seen before. I remember
thinking there and then, that if I could get a guarantee that I

would have a 'Danish' child, I would sign up for having kids tomorrow.

Many years later I got pregnant with my daughter, and I was put on bed rest for four and a half months. During that time, I read countless parenting books, trying to prepare myself for what felt like the scariest journey of my life. A funny thing happened, though, after she was born. I found myself preferring the advice of my Danish family and friends to anything I had read in books. Their suggestions always made more sense – and, more importantly, they worked. Eventually, I stopped consulting parenting books, and 'the Danish way' everyone around me seemed to know about became my official parenting philosophy.

Then one day, while reading the newspaper, I saw that Denmark had been voted the happiest country in the world by the OECD (Organisation for Economic Co-operation and Development). And not only that year – for over forty years in a row they had always been in the top three. I was flabbergasted. I'm American, and my country is obsessed with happiness. There are thousands of books and programmes devoted to the subject. 'The pursuit of happiness' is literally written into the US's Declaration of Independence – and yet we generally score pretty low on the happiness scales. What was Denmark's secret to success, and why didn't more people know about it?

At that moment, a light bulb came on in my head. *It must be the parenting*, I thought. Happy children grow up to be happy adults who raise happy children, and it is a cycle that simply repeats itself. It had changed me so much as a parent – and as a person – I knew it could help others.

I asked a friend and Danish psychotherapist if a guide to the Danish way of parenting existed, and to her knowledge it didn't. And so, together, we uncovered and defined the main tenets of the Danish way of parenting in the acronym PARENT (Play, Authenticity, Reframing, Empathy, No Ultimatums and Togetherness and Hygge).

The PARENT theory is now well established, and our book *The Danish Way of Parenting* has been published in over thirty-three countries, taught in universities, cited in numerous academic papers and – most importantly – used as a trusted resource for parents around the globe. It is based on many years of research, supporting studies and information about the Danish school system and government, along with the personal and professional experience of parents, psychologists and teachers. Most people say it's not just a book for parents but also one for grandparents, teachers, people working with children and non-parents alike.

But how do I put the theory into practice?

Two of the questions I am asked over and over again when I give talks and run workshops are: 'Will it really work for people who don't live in Denmark' and 'I love the theory but how do I put it into practice?' The answer to that first question is *yes*! You see, I didn't live in Denmark for many years while raising my children. I know first-hand how hard it is to change your default settings and cultural beliefs when faced with everyday parenting challenges in another country. However, this is precisely why I know it works!

The second question is partly responsible for this book. It inspired me to want to create a comprehensive guide that describes the Danish parenting model in more detail, offering insights into how Danes get their children to do chores, cook together and settle into bedtime routines and much more. It explores how they deal with toddler meltdowns, teen conflicts, and that looming question on so many people's mind these days: what about screen time? I asked my friend Camilla Semlov Andersson, a Danish family therapist with over twenty-five years of experience working with the Danish Way, to help me conceptualise all the advice, activities, philosophy and tips into a road map for anyone, anywhere in the world. The PARENT model has helped me enormously and continues to help countless parents across the globe. We hope it will help you, too.

The PARENT model: a recap

For those who are unfamiliar with *The Danish Way of Parenting*, here is a recap of the PARENT model.

Play

Play has been considered an educational theory in Denmark since 1871. It is seen as the most important activity a child can engage in. It is the way a child naturally learns, unwinds and even processes their days. Play has been proven to teach some of the most important life skills, including empathy, critical thinking, creativity, self-control and resilience. It also helps us to develop negotiation skills and to learn coping mechanisms that help us deal with stress. In many places, play has been stripped out of schools and homes and replaced with more academic and adult-led activities. At the same time, we have seen an increase in anxiety and depression in many countries, and studies suggest that the two are correlated.

By allowing children more time for unstructured play, we

reduce stress, create more connection and foster wellbeing. The key is to believe in the incredible power of play, as they do in Denmark, and to let go of the belief that children have to 'prove' to adults that they are learning. This reduces stress all around, allows children to learn naturally and makes families happier.

Authenticity

Danes are extremely honest with their children about all aspects of life. This includes talking about all topics in an honest and age-appropriate way and letting them know that all emotions are OK. There are no good or bad emotions, there are only emotions, and we must learn about all of them. Authenticity means being honest with ourselves first and foremost, and then with our children, not sugar-coating life. When children learn that all emotions are normal and that they can trust how they feel, their internal compasses become stronger and calibrated with their own truth north.

Children don't need perfect parents; they need emotionally honest ones. Authenticity is also very much tied to the way we praise our kids. Humility is a huge value in Denmark and Danish parents aim to praise for the effort involved rather than the result so that kids know the goal is the process of mastery, not the label of being a master. Studies show that children who are praised too much for their results or for being 'smart' can become insecure because they are afraid to make mistakes or lose their 'smart' status. Children who are praised for the work they do, however, tend to keep going despite setbacks and failure and are more resilient.

Reframing

Reframing is all about finding the positive details in an otherwise negative situation, changing our use of negative labels and using less black-and-white language. The words we use affect how we feel. Reframing is not about wearing rose-coloured glasses, and it's not denying that negativity exists; it's just seeing better aspects to focus on.

Most of what we believe about ourselves, for example, typically comes from our childhoods: 'I am not good at maths,' 'I am lazy,' etc. These are often labels that our parents unwittingly gave us – and then we go on to do the same with our own children: 'She isn't athletic,' 'He is so aggressive,' 'She is lazy.' What we don't realise is that these labels often become self-fulfilling prophecies. Kids think that if their parents say they are this way, they must *be* this way. Reframing is all about avoiding negative labels, separating children from behaviours, and building up the positive storyline instead. Rather than saying, 'He is so stubborn,' we could say, 'He is so determined.' Rather than saying, 'I hate my mother-in-law,' you could say, 'I don't always get along with her, but she is great with the kids.'

Reframing takes practice, but it is such a useful skill when we are able to find and focus on the better details in a seemingly negative situation. This is true in parenting, work, and in our relationships with ourselves and other people. We have to learn to reframe, but our children will grow up doing it naturally, and this can make a profound difference to their feelings of happiness and wellbeing.

Empathy

Empathy is the ability to put yourself in another person's shoes, and it is closely tied to wellbeing. We are all born with the capacity for empathy, but we have to learn how to hook up the wires. Denmark has been voted one of the most empathetic countries in the world, because empathy is considered one of the most important elements a parent can instil in their child's language and behaviour. From the ages of three to sixteen, empathy is taught in Danish schools, with the aim of helping children to understand all emotions, to be able to feel what someone else feels, and to look for the good in others.

Empathy is about acknowledging how our children are feeling and helping them put their emotions into words rather than discounting them. We can improve how empathetic we are at any age, and it can help us to achieve everything from improved happiness to success in business. As empathy operates on the same neural pathways as forgiveness, it is key for fostering healthy, meaningful relationships.

No ultimatums

In Denmark, the parenting style is very democratic. This is the opposite of authoritarian style, which is the controlling 'my way or the highway' approach commonly used in many countries. Danes do not want their children to fear them in any way. Spanking has been illegal for over twenty-five years and is an unthinkable way to educate children in Denmark. Yelling, screaming and ultimatums are also avoided because they foster fear rather than respect.

Danes see the role of a parent as that of a lighthouse

rather than a warden. They send clear, consistent signals to their children so that they can learn to navigate their life's journey. The 'no ultimatums' approach helps parents to avoid power struggles and reduces the likelihood of immediately going into conflict with their kids. It's about looking for ways to find win/win solutions, rather than win/lose outcomes where, often, everyone loses out. Governing with fear fosters fear, not respect. Often, it's just about being aware of the core values you want to instil (this is what I often refer to as the big lines of parenting), setting kind but firm boundaries and using considerate language and tone. The motto is: 'Teach respect, be respectful and you will be respected.'

Togetherness and hygge

Hygge originates from the old Norse word *hygga*, which means 'to comfort'. It is about cosying around together, but more than that, it is about *being aware* that cosy time is sacred and treating it as such. It is essentially drama-free togetherness time. Hygge is much more than a physical space; it's more of a psychological space that we carve out for ourselves and for the family.

Try to imagine entering this hygge space with your child or family – perhaps as you're having dinner, playing together or taking a walk – and leaving all your stress, complaining, anger and negativity at the door before entering, just as you take off your coat and your shoes. Doing this creates a much-needed oasis and refuge away from the stresses of life. You can be stressed in every other moment, but for these moments, you aim to be *there*. It's not 'me' time, it's 'we' time, and for many cultures this doesn't come naturally. In short, this psychological space provides a shelter from the outside world, and children absolutely love to spend drama-free time with their parents. The more you practise it, the easier it gets. Hygge is not mindfulness – it's '*we*-fulness'.

How to use this book

The PARENT green script

Parenting is one of the hardest jobs in the world. On top of trying to be the person we would like to be for our kids, we also have to keep our households running. So often, this can feel like an constant grind. Calling to mind the Greek myth of Sisyphus, who is forced to continuously push a rock up a hill, these tasks can feel tedious and tend to frequently fall on the shoulders of one parent. We pull our children along, hoping they will behave without incident. We offer them entertainment and distraction in order to allow us to be more efficient and get the tasks done without interruption, or we unwittingly boss them around with threats and ultimatums.

While this is completely understandable, especially when we are tired and stressed, it can also be an unconscious default setting. All of us have been raised with certain perceptions about the role of the parent–child relationship from our own cultures and upbringing. Historically, children have been seen as smaller and less competent than adults, and therefore it's believed that they should obey adults at all costs. It's more of a subject–object relationship. Due to these unconscious beliefs, it's easy to fall into the habit of yelling or demanding, because that was what was normal for many of us when we were growing up.

The Danish Way, on the other hand, is based on seeing children as completely competent from a very early age, and as individuals who need to be listened to and included in conversations in order for them to cooperate. It's a subject–subject relationship, rather than one based on power ('You do what I say because I have the power'). There is no question that, as adults, we have the power, but it's how we use that power that matters. Danish parents feel they have a responsibility to use their power responsibly by treating children with equal dignity rather than as objects. This is a cycle of respect that comes back to you. It's not always easy, though, when you haven't been raised this way, so having a sort of 'emotional script' to fall back on in order to guide us can be incredibly helpful.

Alfred Hitchcock, the famous writer and director of countless movies, was known for making two scripts when he wrote his films. One was called the 'blue script' and one was called the 'green script'. The blue script described what would physically happen in the film, and the green script described what he wanted the audience to feel.

This is a very interesting way to reframe how we see our everyday activities, routines and chores as parents. What if we were to think of our to-do lists as the blue script – what needs to get done – and our 'to-be' lists as the green script – how we ideally want to be/feel with our children.

The Danish Way Every Day aims to help parents develop their green script whenever possible.

The book is divided into three sections: Everyday Activities, Routines and Fun.

Each chapter begins with a common parenting pitfall, followed by an overview of the chapter based around the PARENT model – our green script – to help set the stage and mentally prepare you for the tasks ahead. Every topic then lays out simple activities, language tips, ways to avoid meltdowns, ideas for reframing, ways to encourage empathy, hygge tips and many insights into the Danish parenting philosophy. We will cover:

toddlers (0–3)
young children (4–6)
older children (7–10)
tweens and teens (11–16)

You can either read the whole book in its entirety, or flip to the sections that apply to your child/children. It is recommended that you read the introductions and at least two age groups at a time, along with the PARENT tips, as age group behaviours often overlap depending on where you live.

Research shows that the quality of the time you spend with your children is more important than the quantity. So many parents berate themselves for not doing enough, but even if you can find only ten or twenty minutes a day to dedicate to being present with your kids, it's enough. And if you can't, that's OK too. The important thing is to try. I would like parents to see everyday activities not as obstacles but rather opportunities to embrace quality time. There is no magic wand when it comes to parenting, but the Danish Way really does work. The key is that it's not just about the *doing* that matters; what's important is the *being* together. This is a mindset shift that can be adopted anywhere in the world. It just takes some awareness and a little creative intention to implement it.

I want to clarify that Denmark is not a utopia, and the parenting style is not the only reason the Danes are so happy. Like every country, they have their own internal challenges to deal with, and there are certainly unhappy people living there as well. However, I have simply had the opportunity to see the world through very different lenses – 'Danish lenses', if you will – and it has completely changed my perspective on life. I want to offer you these Danish glasses so you can try them on for yourself – and if you see anything differently, it will have been a success.

PART 1

EVERYDAY ACTIVITIES

As parents, we often believe that spending quality time with our kids means taking expensive trips or going on special outings, but this couldn't be further from the truth. In Denmark, most parents make a big effort to transform everyday activities into opportunities to connect, collaborate and create hygge, rather than seeing them as obstacles. It's not about what *I* have to get done, but rather what we can do *together*. It's about seeing the family as a team, one in which everyone has a role to play. Danes are very aware that from an early age, children love being with their moms and dads – helping out, imitating and playing – and that the sooner we include them, the better.

Cooking, shopping, eating and doing chores together not only improves family bonds, but it also gives kids a chance to feel like they're contributing to the family. Danish parents believe this is very meaningful for children. It fosters a deep sense of self-esteem because kids feel genuinely valued and needed. In a Harvard Grant study that is one of the longest-running longitudinal studies in history (spanning seventy-five years from 1930 to the present) researchers uncovered two things that people need in order to be successful. The first is love and the second is work ethic. According to the experiences of 724 high-achievers who were part of the study, they agreed that a 'pitch-in' mindset and doing chores as a child were key to success. Learning to work well as part of a team is beneficial for our entire lives: at home, in school, at work and in love.

Children who are taken seriously in everyday activities reap numerous benefits. This kind of involvement significantly reduces depression, anxiety and other mental illnesses. It improves vocabulary and problem-solving skills. Children do better in school and have fewer behavioural problems. This time together provides an outlet for pent-up emotions kids may not be able to express otherwise and helps them to process these feelings.

The reality is, we are happier when we see work as a free choice rather than a forced chore. In this way, daily tasks become more fun and meaningful. We are playing on the same team with the shared goal of taking care of each other respectfully. This is far more motivating for everyone. By calibrating our mindset with our parenting green script – how we want *to be* with our children, rather than what we *have to do* – we can move in the direction of more joy and wellbeing for the whole family.

Chores

Parenting pitfall: Making the house a hotel

I started a little late when it came to getting my children involved in helping at home, and it was something I really regretted. I'd had such an aversion to chores growing up that I ended up creating a hotel environment where I did everything for them, robbing them of important lessons in taking care of themselves and contributing to the family. Over time, I started to question my views on chores and why I saw them so negatively. In Denmark, they believe that children naturally want to contribute to the family, and that we are depriving them if we don't include them. From a very early age, Danish children are involved in all aspects of work and play. Every school has a fully functioning kitchen and woodworking rooms where kids do 'chores' or *dukse* together, and education is not just about academics, but also learning how to be a contributing member of society. This is seen as fun for kids. According to the Center for Parenting Education, children who regularly do chores are better able to deal with frustration and delayed gratification, have higher self-esteem and are more responsible than those who don't do chores.

So, what if I changed my approach to be more like that of the Danish Way? What if I saw chores as something playful and an opportunity to be together? And what if I treated the kids as valuable and respected team members? My husband and I talked a lot about making some deliberate changes at home. We were moving house and changing our work situations, so it was a perfect opportunity to signal a new system. We spoke to our children and expressed our need to help each other as a family. Things like cooking, food shopping, doing laundry and weekly cleaning had to become more of a joint effort. I think it was a bit strange for the kids at first, but I know they appreciated feeling that they were being taken more seriously. We made agreements and wrote down how we could each contribute. I worked very hard on myself to stop expecting chores to be done *now*, in exactly the way I wanted them done, and disciplined myself to speak more respectfully – to be less bossy and less demanding. I had to be patient. I often adopted the role of helping them out when I wanted something done, which was new for me. Sometimes I had to remind the kids of our agreements, but things really began to shift in a big way. I was so shocked; I could hardly believe it. I started getting back the respectful treatment I had been giving. This felt like a huge parenting win for me, and I was so incredibly proud. It definitely took some time, but it worked. If I had adopted this approach when they were younger, it would have been so much easier, but it's never too late to change.

PARENT tips

Play

From early on in school, we are taught that work is something we *have* to do, while play is something we *want* to do. Work is hard; play is fun. But in Denmark, work and play are not opposites. When we think of 'work' as play, or as something fun, it brings out our better qualities and makes us feel good. Start kids as early as possible, including them in chores or using parallel play. This could be encouraging them to symbolically sweep up crumbs with a small brush, or 'organising' Tupperware in the kitchen. Danes send the message that chores are something we do together as a family. It's not playtime, but it can be playful, which makes it nicer. Put on some music, dance around and gamify tasks (Who can get all the spots off the window? Who can find the missing socks?). It is much easier to include children when they are young and more likely to be interested than when they become less interested as teenagers. Their interest has a lot to do with your attitude. If you make the experience playful, it will be more fun. If it seems like drudgery, it will be. Play, by definition, is something you are always free to quit. If you can't quit and have no choice, it is no longer play. Remember that nothing sucks the joy out of work like having no freedom to choose or dealing with a micromanaging boss.

Authenticity

It's OK if it's not perfect! Accept the effort made and the job done. Focus on what your child does right, rather than pointing out what they do wrong. Think about how you would feel if someone asked you to help, then criticised your efforts and did the whole thing again 'the right way' once you were done. Subtle messages sent by redoing work can erode confidence. This is true for all chores. Aim to praise kids for the work they've done and their general helpfulness, rather than picking apart their efforts. They are learning and this is part of the process. We want kids to feel genuinely needed, valued and appreciated, and we can help them learn by doing tasks together. Help them fold. Help them vacuum. Use 'we' and 'let's' instead of 'you', so it feels like a joint experience. If they feel valued, they will be more intrinsically motivated to help than if they are faced with extrinsic threats or offered bribes. Feeling valued will develop their true sense of personal responsibility. Also, we as parents aren't always the neatest and cleanest, and it's OK to be honest about that: 'I know I can be messy too. This is why I try to remember to clean up straight away so it doesn't build up more.' Honesty and vulnerability are far better than hypocrisy. We are all trying our best, and doing chores is just one of those things we do as a family unit.

Reframing

Learn to see chores as something we choose to do, not something we have to do. Seeing chores as a choice (and something you can enjoy) makes all the difference to how you experience it. This is how you can hone a child's natural desire to contribute. Whether the task is helping put dishes in the dishwasher, doing laundry together or tidying up, it can be seen as an extension of the child's play – but the reframe needs to come from you. For all ages, doing chores can be a really nice way to spend time together. Younger kids love to be with us, while for older kids, it can be a wonderful opportunity for chats we wouldn't have otherwise. Like driving, doing the dishes or tidying up offers a way to focus on a task that doesn't involve eye contact, which can be the catalyst for great conversations.

Mess can be very triggering, and sometimes, as parents, we may instantaneously call our kids 'lazy', 'spoilt' or 'messy'. Calling kids names isn't going to motivate them. If we start out with an attitude of annoyance and expectation, we very often promote the very behaviour we don't want – and that's a sure way to go into a power struggle. The more we are able to see our children's positive sides and understand them (depending on their age, brain development and what can be expected) the more we can act with respect. Reframe your attitude and use humour whenever possible: 'Is that a science project you're growing in your room? Can we clean it up or do you need it for class?' Another way of Danish reframing is to externalise a negative label. So, instead of saying, 'You are so lazy and messy,' you could say, 'We can all be struck by bouts of "laziness" and "messy moments" – adults included.' This shows your child that these are not fixed traits, and they don't define us as people.

Empathy

It used to be believed that kids were not empathetic, but this is simply not true. Studies show that toddlers naturally help out when they see an adult in need of assistance. Eighteen-month-olds will almost always try to help an adult who is struggling with a task. If the adult is reaching for something, the toddler will try to hand it to them, and if they see them drop something, they will pick it up. This is why involving young children in daily tasks is setting them up to be natural helpers for life. As they get older, they may not feel like helping sometimes, and this is normal. Consider how they are spending their time: are they lounging on the sofa, or doing homework or practising an instrument? Cleaning doesn't have to be a test to see whether they jump at your beck and call. If you like the way they are using their time and they don't take things for granted, you can be flexible. Also, it's fine to have preferences. Would they rather do outdoor tasks, like taking out the bins, or indoor tasks, like cleaning the kitchen or feeding pets? We all have things we need to do as a family, but not everyone needs to do everything.

No ultimatums

Aftaler or agreements are powerful and widely used in Denmark to help avoid power struggles. These agreements are a core part of chores, because they ensure that everyone understands what needs to be done, what the expectations are and who is responsible for what. For example, your agreements around chores might be: 'In our family, we help each other. That's how our family works. We do tasks together.'

Get your kids to commit to helping. You might say, 'I really need help setting the table and with the vacuuming today. Are you OK with doing it?' The more kids are involved in this understanding and participate in the agreements from early on, the less you will have to use ultimatums. Instead, you can communicate respectfully: 'We agreed your room would be cleaned up today. When do you think you can do it? After this show? OK.' These agreements can be made daily or weekly, at breakfast or at special family meetings. They might be verbal agreements or a written list stuck on the fridge detailing who will do what – different approaches will work for different families. What's most important is that the children are involved and included in these agreements, and that their preferences are acknowledged. The feeling of being valued and having a voice builds self-worth and a sense of personal responsibility, which is an intrinsic motivator rather than an extrinsic one, such as getting a reward for helping or being punished if they don't.

Togetherness and hygge

Chores in themselves can be a really nice time to cosy around together if you learn to see them that way, and you can also use togetherness in your rewards. Some Danes award physical rewards like stickers for doing chores, but rather than a reward being about something material, it could be more about working towards being together in hygge: doing things like going to the zoo, taking a walk in the woods, or making their favourite dinner. It's a careful balance; you don't want 'rewards' to become something that is *expected* in return for doing chores.

Embracing minimalism is another way to focus on what really matters, and it's a very popular approach in Denmark. Less clutter, more hygge. Try to declutter often, getting rid of things you don't need and toys they don't use. This has a host of mental benefits, helping to clear the mind and foster creativity.

Let kids have their own space in the living room (*hygge krog* or 'hygge corner') that is respected so they feel a part of the family space and it's clear where their things can go.

Chores with toddlers (0–3)

Start young: imitation and inclusion

Danes know that it's very easy to get younger children to participate, so doing tasks together can start as soon as possible. Most parents will find that, once they start cleaning, little children naturally gravitate towards being with them, and then it becomes easier to suggest something they can help with and teach new skills. Being part of the cleaning can be great fun for toddlers. It's part of their play. For example, they can:

- use their own sponge or cloth so they can imitate you as you clean

- wash windows that are at their height with natural solution and a small squeegee
- use a very small dustpan and brush to get into corners while we sweep the floor
- tidy things into baskets you hold out for them
- hand you things as you work (asking them for these items also builds vocabulary)
- help you load and unload the washing machine or dryer
- sort socks and clothing by colour
- help hang up clothes to dry – if the clothes line or dryer is at their height – or hand them to you from the basket

Parallel play

Very young ones can be included by engaging in parallel play next to us – whether that's sorting clothes pegs, using a small brush to symbolically 'help' us sweep, or rearranging Tupperware while we clean the kitchen. These are all ways to foster inclusion from early on in play.

Child sight

In Danish there is a word, *barnesyn*, which literally means 'child sight'. It means seeing the world through a child's eyes. Danes use this expression to help them see their children's worlds emotionally and physically. Try to get down on the floor and see the physical world through your toddler's eyes. Is there anything they can reach? Are the sockets covered? Are there any wires or power cords that they could trip on? Is there clutter or mess on the floor? Is it clear to them where things should be put away? Toddlers like things to have a place and to know where that place is. And when we know the area is safe, we can relax more when tidying up and playing with them, and when enjoying family hygge.

Setting up a hygge home

Scandinavian households tend to be very minimalist. Reducing the amount of stuff and clutter makes organisation for children and adults easier. By giving them special boxes, drawers or shelves in the living room and their bedrooms for putting their things away, and perhaps by creating a 'hygge corner' with a teepee and toys, Danish parents make their children feel like a part of the household, not separate from it. Here are some ways you can give your children a sense of having their own space and being part of the home.

- Create a hygge corner in the living room using a teepee, a small rug, a basket with some toys and books, and a comfy bean bag.
- Have a specific spot for everything. Small bookcases with space for boxes that can be easily removed are a great way for your kids to store their favourite toys.
- Set up a play kitchen where they can engage in parallel play.
- If possible, furnish their bedroom with a small closet with drawers, shelves and hangers that they can reach, so that they can be part of taking clothes out and putting them away.
- Try to keep the quantity of toys and clothes that are in their spaces minimal and seasonal, changing them out as the seasons change. This reduces clothing battles and fosters more creativity.

- In the bathroom, add a low step so they can reach the
  sink, a laundry basket for dirty clothes and towels, and
  a low hook where they can hang their own towel.

It's perhaps not surprising, given its Scandinavian origins,
but IKEA is a good source of affordable solutions for the
Scandinavian hygge home from a child's point of view.

Chores with young children (4–6)

Break it into small tasks

If you make cleaning and tidying part of a daily routine, it's
easier to make it part of afternoon play. This way, it doesn't
get so overwhelming that it takes hours, and it's easier to
include your child. Try to create a routine built up of small
tasks, like:

- straightening the cushions
- hanging up clothes
- making the bed
- putting away toys
- watering plants or tending to the garden

🧦 Togetherness matters 🧦

The main thing to remember with young children is to try
to do things together so the child doesn't feel alone in the

activity. Remember: 'In our family, we help each other. That's how our family works. We do tasks together.' It's always more pleasant to do things together, rather than alone. It's impossible to overstate how important this philosophy is when it comes to chores and household duties in general, and what a difference it makes for kids of this age – and often for older kids, too.

Make chores playful

Putting on music, singing and dancing can be a very helpful way to get a playful vibe going and make cleaning up more appealing for everyone – including ourselves! Cleaning together can be entertaining and playful for children. Always remember that they like to be with us, especially when we are in a fun mood. The earlier we take advantage of their innate desire to join in, the more successfully we will plant the seeds for long-term helpers. Invite them to help. For example:

- give children special areas to dust, clean and be responsible for
- encourage them to stand on a ladder or stool and clean the kitchen counter or table
- do the dishes together
- have them put their toys away and tidy their hygge corner
- let them help with vacuuming if they are able to hold and manoeuvre the vacuum cleaner

Focus on effort, not perfection

For some of us, constant correcting is a habit we've inherited from our own parents. This can negate what we are trying to encourage: the child feeling like a useful contributing part of the *fællesskab* (family community). When our kids help us, let's show our gratitude and remember to live with areas that are not as perfectly clean as we would like them to be. Be grateful for the effort they've put in. We can help them learn to get better at cleaning as we work together – use 'we' and 'let's' more than 'you'. For example:

> 'Oh, we missed a spot here.'
> 'Let me help you with that so we get the whole carpet.'
> 'Let's fold these towels together. We try to make the corners match, like this.'

Chores with older children (7–10)

Don't mix love with business

There is nothing wrong with kids having regular chores, but don't mix love with business. Danes want kids to understand that we help each other because we are a family, and the child's efforts are appreciated – but chores aren't completed in exchange for love. Chores have nothing to do with love. They are part of what we do to keep our family running together, and everyone has an important role to play. We want to foster goodwill and personal responsibility, but much like the grades they achieve at school, your child completing chores has nothing to do with how much you love them, or how much they love you.

Increase responsibility

If children have been helping out over the years, they can now begin to take almost complete responsibility for some aspects of cleaning. And, as parents, we can help them, exactly as they have helped us in the rest of the house. In this way, we really show that we are a team.

For example, children of this age can assume a leading role in:

- doing the dishes and loading/unloading the dishwasher
- cleaning their rooms and making their beds
- folding and putting away their clothing
- taking care of pets
- vacuuming and sweeping
- cleaning windows that they can safely reach
- cleaning bathrooms
- taking out trash
- dusting
- setting and clearing the table
- cooking
- watering and tending to plants
- sorting and doing their laundry

The democratic approach to chores

Following through on agreements is very important, but Danes generally try to avoid threats and ultimatums for not following through. They trust children will get it, as long as they believe in them and keep including them. Taking away screen time might help you win in the short term, but it won't help in the long run, as the goal is to build up a sense of personal responsibility rather than obedience. Personal responsibility comes from feeling respected and feeling that your contribution is needed. Obedience is doing what you are told out of fear or because of threats. It's an important difference. Communicating with your child with respect also helps set you up for the teenage years to come. If you are harsh, your child will reflect your attitude later on. If you are respectful, this will also be reflected. Keep that in mind.

Try using phrases like: 'I am just asking when you can clean up, because it means a lot to me. Is there something we can do to make it easier for you to remember the agreements we've made? I know you want to help, but then something comes up and you forget. Shall we plan to clean up after breakfast, and then you can play?'

Help them understand natural consequences

We can let children know that we are disappointed that we had to do something alone.

You might say: 'You said you were going to help me. I reminded you, and now I'm late and stressed, and that's why I am not in a good mood. Will you please remember to help me next time?'

This approach shows them how hard it is for you and demonstrates that there are natural consequences – being late and feeling stressed – when you have to do things alone.

Cultural differences and consequences

For some parents, it's too hard to not have consequences; it's just too far from their starting point culturally. If it's too much of a stretch for you to work with full democracy, at least try to have the sanctions come from your child so they have been a part of the decision. Ask them: 'If you didn't follow through on what we agreed, what do you think is a fair consequence?'

Chores with tweens and teens (11–16)

Treat them like small adults

Teens can help out with all manner of cleaning tasks if they have been shown how. It is a good idea to tell your teen when you need the job to be done by instead of telling them that you need it done now or shortly. Talk to them as you would your partner and give them some say in deciding when they can do it. For example:

'We need to clean the house. When will be best for you?'
'I can see you are busy with your friends, but in an hour I need help preparing the table.'
'Next weekend, we are having a big dinner with family and friends. I really need some help, so could you put it into your schedule that Saturday is our cleaning day.'
'I don't want to interrupt you, but we agreed you would clean up today. When can you do it? After this show? OK.'

Allowance

At this age many kids do earn an allowance or pocket money in Denmark (and some do much earlier), but it is not universal. Money isn't a reward for helping per se; it's so kids can have something of their own to spend. Helping out in the house is still considered something we do as a family, and not something they should be paid for. This is really up to you to decide, but kids understand money much more at this age and may have some special things they want to save up for. It's also very common for teens to have part-time jobs.

Be aware of the distinction between family work and work

There is a distinction between nice family bonding activities and more hardcore cleaning jobs. In many cases, you need to be aware of the different kinds.

For example, dragging dirty, stinking trash out to bins is work, not family bonding time, but laying the table and setting out plates and glasses is nice to do together. Light cleaning and tidying up is a nice task; scrubbing the bathroom floor and cleaning the toilet is work.

Harder work can be tied to an award like an allowance. There are two benefits to this. One, it's an early lesson in how life works. And two, it requires an agreement, like a work contract. Don't get hung up on forcing unpleasant work just to test them to make sure they do their duties.

Building a new system

If you haven't been including your tween or teen in the cleaning up until now it will be difficult – but not impossible – to change. It's good to take the time to explain why things are changing if you're implementing a new system. Children who have never been asked to help before will of course resist (why wouldn't they?). Perhaps you need to have some family meetings to discuss changes that mean you really need their help in the house. Maybe one or both parents are going back to work; perhaps the cleaning person can't come any more; maybe there is a house move coming up, or other changes in the family. Having your partner on board for these meetings is paramount, so that it's clear this is a team decision to move in a new direction.

🥾 Make a plan together 🥾

Be clear and explain what needs to be done and why. The idea is always the same: 'We are a team, and our family works together as a unit to make it work.' It's all about involvement and agreements. Be clear about how you help them, and how they can help. It's a system. Make a list together of all the things that need to be done in the house, and decide who wants to do what and when, from week to week or day to day.

Choose your battles wisely

It is inevitable that there will be times when your kids do not want to help out, and this is totally normal. Remember your big lines of parenting and choose your battles wisely. Perhaps your child is busy with homework or enjoying a hobby they are passionate about. Do you feel their help is absolutely fundamental right now? This doesn't mean getting into the habit of doing all the cleaning by yourself – absolutely not – but it's OK to be respectful of their interests if you like how they are using their time. When you are respectful of your children and their time, they will often reward you with respect in turn.

A room of their own

You can consider your tween or teen's room as their domicile. It is their place. As long as their room is not a health hazard, then try to respect their limits. Do they really need to have a clinically cleaned-up room? Mess is less important than whether they are thriving in their room, and if the way they keep it works for them in terms of keeping track of their things, then respect that. It doesn't have to be cleaned in exactly the way you would do it if it were your room. If they have books in a pile by the bed, despite having a bookshelf, this could be OK if it's what works for them. If they have a creative hobby they enjoy, then it might be fine for them to leave the materials they use for it out on the desk or table. Even if you think it would be obvious and neater to put them away, it may be better for them to leave them out. Let them make their own systems. If you can see that their room is a huge mess because they don't know how to keep it or are not able to get a system going, then you can offer to help them, so it feels like a joint effort rather than a command. In this way, you show them that you respect their inner space (what's going on for them inside) and their outer space too.

Make a kind gesture

Your teen may be acting moody, rude or grumpy, and you may be fed up with their mess, but try to look for the reasons for their behaviour. They may be:

- having a hard time at school
- having difficulties with friends
- feeling overwhelmed with activities
- feeling stressed about schoolwork or tests

Surprise them once in a while by tidying up, changing their sheets, doing laundry or helping out with some chore they are behind on. Don't do it with strings attached, expecting loads of gratitude; just do it quietly, maybe offering a hug. You can do it with them or alone. It shouldn't become a hotel service, but you will be surprised how much teens appreciate these gestures of kindness.

Respect their time

Remember that tweens and teens have *a lot* going on in their brains and their worlds; the more we understand this, the more we can reframe their behaviour as bouts of laziness (rather than engrained traits) or moments of forgetfulness.

For teens, it's better to get an agreement on when they want to do chores. Try to adjust your expectations depending on what's happening in their lives. This communicates respect for their time, and fosters a sense of personal responsibility.

🧦 Some more tips for tweens and teens 🧦

- If you want less conflict, treat your teen in a more equal way.
- Remember tweens and teens have a lot on their plates and can forget to complete chores.
- Prioritise teaching personal responsibility over obedience. Be patient. Think about the quality of your relationship rather than your desire for perfectly done chores.
- Don't punish unless the consequences were agreed. Would you sanction or punish your partner?
- Help them out and make it a joint effort if they don't have time or energy. This can also be an opportunity to be together and talk.

Shopping

Parenting pitfall:
Not tuning in to myself or my child

One of my biggest parenting regrets comes from an incident that took place when my son was three years old and we went to the supermarket. I was so determined to spend 'quality' time together that day that I was not at all tuned in to myself or to him. The reality was I was completely exhausted, with no surplus energy, and the same was true for him. We were both very tired from work and day care, but I was so determined to 'make it work' that I didn't realise I was setting us up for the opposite of what I wanted. By the time we reached the checkout, I was extremely frustrated. I had planned for us to have a hot chocolate afterwards, and was determined to get to it quickly so we could get through our 'quality time'. Then I had to hurry up and make dinner. I wasn't really being present, and my son knew it. He had stopped to look at something in the stationery aisle and wanted to show it to me; thinking he just wanted to buy a toy, I immediately yelled at him to come over right now and stop looking, adding, 'And no, we are not going to buy that!'

He became more and more resistant as I insisted, and this escalated into a full-on temper tantrum. I had to take him out of the store and carry him kicking and screaming to the car. So much for quality time. He screamed the whole way home, kicking and lashing out, and I ended up screaming back at him. I felt so horrible and ashamed of my own behaviour. Looking back, I realise that I just didn't have the energy for that outing. I thought it was him who wasn't listening to me, but in truth, it was me who wasn't listening to him. He had just wanted to show me a picture of a tiger on a notebook in the stationery aisle. I could have acknowledged what he was showing me, rather than accusing him of wanting something. I could have tried to include him in a task, like putting the groceries on the belt, or given him something else entirely to play with from the start, knowing that – in truth – I just wasn't in the right state of mind. If I had simply tuned in to myself – and him – I could have completely changed this scene for the better.

PARENT tips

Note: Examples in this chapter are based on grocery shopping but can be adjusted to apply to other shopping scenarios too.

Play

Ask yourself: 'How can I make the shopping trip more playful?' Depending on your child's age, you might consider whether there is something you can put in the shopping trolley that they can sit with and play with that you'll feel OK about? In Denmark, most supermarkets also have child-sized trolleys that they can push so they feel like part of it. Try setting up the shopping experience so that your child feels in control and taken seriously. Give them a task; ask them to cross items off the list, or fill their own shopping trolley. Make grocery-store scavenger hunts: look for items with different colours or shapes, or belonging to different food groups. For older kids, you can play estimation games based around budgeting for meals (see page 46). These are fun ways that include kids in the experience and also help them develop a sense of responsibility.

Authenticity

Before you go shopping, ask yourself: 'How much time do I have? And do I have enough surplus energy to make the shopping trip a nice time where the experience becomes time shared with my child in a cosy and *hyggelig* way?' Tune in to how you are really feeling. Are you in a rush, or is your child too tired to engage? Be honest with yourself; perhaps you just need to get it over with. Children are incredible lie detectors and can sense when we are being fake, hiding emotions or 'controlling' the situation rather than collaborating, so try to be as truthful as possible about whether you can go all-in or semi-include them – or whether you need to give them something to keep them occupied while you complete the task. It's absolutely fine whatever you choose, but it's much better to tune in and be emotionally honest.

Reframe

Listen to your parental answering machine. Many parents have the tendency to automatically reprimand, repeating phrases like:

'No!'
'Come on, leave that alone.'
'We aren't buying that.'

'We don't have time.'
'Stop touching that.'

Sound familiar? This is very often just an engrained habit, a cultural default setting based on our own upbringing. We all have a kind of automatic parental answering machine that is programmed into us, made up of a mix of 'received wisdom' we got from our own parents, grandparents and wider society. This answering machine robotically spouts off advisory and 'helpful' comments. Often, this involves referring to ourselves in the third person, for example:

'Mommy said no; don't touch that.'
'Did you hear what Daddy told you about not taking things
   off the shelf?'
'Didn't Mommy just tell you to stop screaming?'

Try to hear your own parental answering machine and pay attention to the things you say without thinking. Notice when you are viewing a situation or your child's behaviour through a negative lens. Take a step back and see if you can change your perspective on the situation. Ask yourself: 'Am I speaking about myself in the third person? Am I moralising or talking *at* my child?'

Remember, at certain ages, children are programmed to seek independence. This is how they learn. In Danish, for example, the toddler age is called *trodsælder*, or 'the boundary-pushing age', not 'the terrible twos' as we usually refer to it in English. Danes see toddlers' boundary-pushing behaviour as healthy and normal, *not* annoying and terrible, and this direct-ly affects how they respond to it. When we see our children as inherently good, we treat them that way.

Empathy

Am I speaking in a way that is taking my child's needs and feelings seriously, or am I discounting them? If a meltdown begins, instead of saying, 'Don't be like that,' or 'Stop it, you have nothing to cry about,' try getting down on their level and acknowledging their emotions.

You might say: 'I see you are upset. What are you upset about? Is it because I didn't stop to look at what you were showing me?'

Remember, there are always good reasons for a child's emotions. This is true for all ages. Think how you would feel as an adult if your feelings were constantly shut down or dismissed as wrong or unnecessary. You would probably have a meltdown, too. By acknowledging their senses and feelings without judgement, rather than ignoring them or discounting them, you are teaching respect, and this respect will come back to you in time.

No ultimatums

Tune in to your child and tune out other people's judgement. Don't look for power struggles, and you won't find them. Think win/win, not *I* win. A good question to ask yourself when you are in a public situation and a conflict starts is: 'Is my reaction focused on how my child is doing (acknowledging their feelings), or is it focused on what I sense other people want (an obedient child)?'

Who is responsible for the quality of your relationship with your child – is it you, or random people in the supermarket? When you claim responsibility for your relationship with your child rather than placing blame on them, you are better able to act respectfully, and this automatically helps avoid power struggles.

Togetherness and hygge

Foster a team mentality: see the family as a team. What can you all contribute (depending on your child's age), and how can you prepare for this? This might include asking your child to:

- think of ideas for meals, lunches and snacks
- make shopping lists
- look for items in the shop
- place the shopping on the conveyor belt at the checkout

Be patient and take their tasks seriously. Mirror what they see and do, and acknowledge observations together with a normal tone, rather than quizzing them for right answers. Going shopping can be an especially nice time to spend together in hygge with toddlers as well as tweens and teens. The key is involvement and inclusion, and the earlier you start, the more natural it becomes as they get older.

Shopping with toddlers (0–3)

Pay attention to what your child is showing interest in

Children are curious and interested in following what is going on around them. When you walk around the store, try registering what they are noticing and excited about. (The mistake I made with my son in the example I gave on page 34 was not paying attention to what had caught his interest.)

Look for the positive storyline

If you find yourself instinctively reprimanding or tugging your toddler away from 'doing something wrong', try to reframe. Are they trying to show you something or communicate with you? Are they trying to help? Toddlers are supposed to push boundaries, which is totally normal and healthy for their age. Very often, these simple reframes can help you respond differently and reduce power struggles.

Imitation and inclusion

Little children love to copy the adult world – to imitate us. Here are some ideas for bringing this into your shopping trip.

- Let them take a smaller trolley of their own to pull or push, if they have one in the grocery store (if you are semi-including them in the shopping, you can put them in the trolley).
- Point to items they can reach and ask them to hand them to you or put them in the trolley.
- Put the fruit or vegetables in a bag together: ask them to hold the bag while you add the items, or vice versa.
- Pick them up to help them reach an item you need from a higher shelf; try describing the colour or what it looks or feels like to see if they can spot the item themselves.
- Let them help put groceries on the checkout belt. Even very young children can help with this.
- Weigh the fruits and vegetables together, letting them push the buttons on the scales.

Avoid overstimulation

Some kids may get energy by shopping together with you. Other kids may become overwhelmed from overstimulation, which can create a meltdown. If you are not sure about your child's energy levels, it's fine to put them in the shopping trolley with a book, earphones and music, or something that allows them to have some alone time in their own world. This helps insulate them from all the noise and surrounding impressions that can cause more sensory overload and acting out.

Help them communicate

Consider how it would feel to view your surroundings and not be able to articulate what you see. Anyone who has studied another language can relate to the feeling you get when you know more than you can express, and it can feel *very* frustrating! By showing interest in what our kids draw our attention to, we can help them express their experiences. This builds core self-esteem because they feel seen, heard and understood.

Practise mirroring

Mirroring is simply observing what children are doing and looking at. It's being with them rather than extracting from them. It's not a quiz. It's following your child's natural exploration process and putting words to it. Danes communicate like this from the time their children are babies to help them articulate their surroundings. Follow your child's interested gaze and merely state back to them what they see, then expand on it. Use your normal voice and tone. For example:

'There's a lot of fruit. Do you see the apples?'
'Oh, you want to take the butter and put it in the trolley?
   Here you go.'
'That pasta bag makes a funny noise when you touch it.
   Can I try?'

Connecting and mirroring their emotions so they feel seen and heard is extremely powerful. Danish children tend to be very mature, and one of the reasons is the way adults communicate with them from an early age. They show kids that they see them and are interested in their observations ('I see *you*, not who I want you to be'). It's a subtle but powerful distinction.

⅜ The Danish way in action ⅜

I vividly remember being at the checkout in a supermarket in Denmark and marvelling at a mom, who was clearly exhausted, with two small toddlers: one was in a pram, aged about one, and the other was standing next to it, and was about two and a half years old. They were both trying to help take out the groceries, which was sweet, but I just sensed a ticking time bomb. One of the toddlers started to crawl on to the conveyor belt and I thought, *Oh no.* I was already reprimanding him in my head: *Stop! Get down!*

The mother quickly came behind him (*Oh lord,* I thought, *now the screaming begins*), but rather than snatching him away from the conveyor belt as I was expecting, she calmly picked him up and held him closer to the groceries.

'Here, sweetie, you can reach them now,' she said. 'Can you hand me the bread? Yes, and that is the fruit.'

He quietly and happily took the products and handed them to her. I couldn't believe it. She saw his behaviour as him just wanting to help, not being naughty. That reframe made such an impression on me. My instinctive reaction to his actions would have surely ended in screaming and tears, and all because I wasn't tuning in to the positive storyline of what he actually wanted to do – help her.

Shopping with young children (4–6)

Let them do it authentically

When you let your child do something, like crossing something out on the grocery list, make sure they really do it, and that you aren't just 'letting' them do it in a fake way. Kids can sense this. Trust them to trust in themselves. See them as capable and confident, and they will feel and become more capable and confident, and will want to help more in future. They will develop an authentic sense of personal responsibility.

For example:

- Let them take the trolley (or pull or push a smaller one, if the store has them).
- Make a list where they write or draw items to buy.
- Ask them to find items on the list, then cross out the words or pictures.
- Let them put the groceries on the conveyor belt.
- Bag the groceries together.

Meltdowns

Supermarkets and shops can be classic places for meltdowns. This can be for a myriad of reasons, from a child not wanting to walk any more to them being hungry. The key is to have the patience and wherewithal to get through those phases and moments without losing your cool, staying focused on what is important. We can't expect our children to keep it cool if *we* lose control. Let's make sure to take our child's needs, desires, experiences and feelings seriously, along with our own. This is a classic parenting pitfall.

Here's an example.

If your three-year-old doesn't want to walk any more, but you have too many groceries in your arms to carry the child as well, you could say: 'I understand you don't want to walk but these bags are so heavy; I can't carry them and you. Shall we rest for a moment until you can walk again?'

In this way, you show your child that you see them and respect them, but you also have boundaries for yourself.

DEALING WITH MELTDOWNS

Imagine there's a long line at the checkout counter. A four-year-old girl pulls on her mother's arm and says desperately, 'Mom! I want to go home. Why can't we go home?'

Here are three ways the girl's parent might handle this:

The 'old-fashioned' way: The mom feels compelled to give her daughter social instructions on how to behave. She pulls her arm away from her daughter and says aggressively, 'No, now stop that and be quiet! When you go into stores, you wait until it's your turn, do you understand me?'

The girl ends up crying.

In this example, the daughter isn't taken seriously. Her mother ignores her feelings and needs. The girl also talks to her mom with a whiny language and complaining voice, which shows she isn't used to being taken seriously. The daughter has learned from early on that her desires and needs are unimportant to her mom and possibly annoying.

The more 'modern' way: The mother democratically asks for her daughter's understanding with an objective observation, but her tone belies the words. She says: 'No, it's not possible to leave right now. I understand that you are hot and tired, but can't you see that there are a lot of people waiting ahead of me?'

In this example, the mother indirectly sends the message that her daughter's feelings and needs are not as important to her as the adults waiting in line, even though she *says* that she understands that she's tired. The daughter is encouraged to take her mother's way of experiencing reality seriously without the mother really reciprocating.

The girl cries quietly.

The Danish way: The mother acknowledges her daughter's feelings, senses and needs, and respectfully looks for 'win/win' rather than 'I win' solutions. She uses a kind voice and responds: 'You're right. It is so hot in here – and look at all these people! I just need to pay for this before we go. Could you please go and put the trolley back over there?'

In this example, there is no power struggle between the mother and her daughter. The daughter goes and puts the trolley back as suggested. She cooperates even though she can't go home immediately as she would have liked. In this case, neither of them 'loses', unlike in the first and second examples. The reason is that the daughter is used to being taken seriously, and she knows that her feelings and needs are acknowledged.

Shopping with older children (7–10)

Increase responsibility

Kids are capable of so much more at this age and can really contribute in a more meaningful way. Giving them a real role in the shopping, depending on their age and if they are in the mood, helps build up many skills and can be a lot of fun.

🦵 Game: Cooking on a budget 🦵

Try coming up with a meal to cook together based on a particular budget. This is a fun way to talk about recipes and different kinds of food, and can help your child investigate food prices and learn maths. As part of this game, your child can:

- choose a recipe and write out a list of what's needed
- estimate the cost of each item
- gather the food on the list
- write the actual costs next to estimated costs on the list
- weigh the vegetables
- put the groceries on the conveyor belt
- bag the groceries
- help unpack the groceries

🧦 Game: Guess the cost 🧦

Give your child a copy of the grocery list and have them estimate how much each item will cost, and how much they think the entire shopping trip will cost. Let them write down the real cost of each item as they find it. They can change the items or make adjustments and substitutions if they think something costs too much. When you're home and all the groceries are put away, give them the receipt so they can compare their estimates to the overall cost.

Ask them:

- How close were your guesses?
- What item prices did you estimate better than others?
- What prices surprised you?
- Could we have substituted anything?
- Why do you think you were so close/so far from the correct answer?

Shopping with tweens and teens (11–16)

Choice versus duty

Some parents make their kids do things because they think it's 'good for them' rather than because they need the help. This is a small difference but an important one. When kids are asked to participate because we need their help, they feel valuable to us. When kids are told to do something because it's 'good for them', they can feel like objects.

Responsibility versus obedience

Being at someone's 'beck and call' and having to do whatever they tell us doesn't feel nice for anyone! Think about how you would feel in this situation. It isn't conducive to feeling valuable. One of the ways we can foster self-esteem and intrinsic motivation is by regularly including kids in the family agreements of what needs to be done and then framing it as a choice, rather than as a duty.

This might mean deciding together on a night when your teen would like to cook for the family (or would like you to help them do so). They can then look up and choose a recipe, make a list of what to buy, and work out their budget. Teens can go to the supermarket on their own to shop for dinner or other food on decided nights of the week. It can still be a team endeavour, because you can help them just as they have helped you. You could say:

'Remember our agreement about going to the grocery
    store and cooking today?'
'Do you have the list? I'll get the other stuff we need.'
'Would you like me to help you cook?'

Cooking

Parenting pitfall: Being the lone martyr

I always thought cooking was my job in the family, and that I just had to get it done. I saw cooking as a form of drudgery and I had a deeply engrained belief that it somehow ultimately fell on my shoulders. Rather than actively looking for ways to include my kids or husband in cooking, it was easier just to say, 'It's fine, I've got it,' while quietly feeling resentful because I was doing so many things on my own. I am not proud of this, but I think many parents can relate. We think it's easier to do it ourselves than to ask for help.

The truth is, many families have a habit of seeing the job of cooking as the role of one person, often the mother. This is typically passed down from previous generations, and even if we question it, we often continue to do it because it feels normal – it's a cultural default setting.

Danes have quite evolved views on 'traditional roles', and as I explored this, I started to really question my engrained beliefs. I worked on reframing my mindset around cooking. I started to see cooking as a family affair, rather than something to be completed as a lone martyr. My husband and I agreed to cook more together, or took turns cooking and involving the kids in little tasks. I saw it as an opportunity to spend quality time together and a moment to enjoy rather than a dreaded chore. I looked for more creative ways to prepare food we liked, rather than just finding something to eat. We gave the kids an occasional 'meal night' to be in charge of, where they worked together to lead the cooking, and we supported them in setting the table or doing assigned tasks. I stopped feeling guilty about asking for help and receiving it, and I also stopped overcorrecting the help when I got it. Of course, there were plenty of times when I didn't have the surplus energy and so just threw something easy in the oven, but changing my beliefs around cooking truly changed my experience. I now find it to be one of the most enjoyable moments to be had together as a family, or even on my own.

PARENT tips

Play

Studies show that the more kids play with food from a very young age – especially while cooking – the more likely they will be to taste and enjoy what they eat, and to be open to and interested in trying new foods. Sensorial play, where you use all the senses, should be at the top of your mind. How can you engage your child's senses of taste, touch, smell, sound and sight?

All kids, from the moment they can sit, can be involved in parallel play, making music or stirring a pretend sauce on the floor. Even a baby that has recently learned to sit on the floor can be with you in the kitchen when you are cooking. At this age, of course, it's important to be aware of keeping a child away from dangerous situations like a hot oven, boiled water, sharp knives, etc, but they can still be in the room with you.

Most exposure to food is good exposure. So even if it's messy, make the cooking process playful and inclusive. For older kids, set up pizza-making, outdoor cooking or engaging activities around food on weekends to keep them included (this can also be a great way to get to know their friends). Just because they are older doesn't mean they can't be involved in the family, and cooking and eating together is the perfect way to include them. Danish kids cook pretty regularly indoors and outdoors from kindergarten onwards, because it is such an integral part of play, hygge and education.

Cooking outdoors can be a great experience to enjoy as a family, whether it's over an open fire or using a portable stove for camping. Try making:

- pancakes
- soup
- *snobrød* dough wrapped around a stick
- popcorn
- toasted marshmallows or s'mores

Authenticity

A big focus of the Danish Way is how you speak to children: as equals, collaborators and helpers rather than as *performers*. It's through the little interactions that we make the biggest differences.

A good question to ask is: 'How can I focus my language on the experience of cooking with my child, rather than praising them for doing tasks for me?' Try saying:

'Wow, you are really concentrating hard on that.'
'Can I help you?'

'I really like being here with you.'

'Can I taste what you are making?'

This doesn't mean never praising them (not at all!); it just means taking a moment to ask yourself:

- Do I need to praise right now, or am I just filling silence or giving empty praise? Do I have to fill this silence, or can I just observe?
- Could I find another way to describe what is happening instead of 'Good job,' where I focus on what they are experiencing? Perhaps, 'That looks fun.'

Reframing

We all come to our adult family lives with beliefs around cooking and 'roles', and it is so important to address these so we can actively reframe. How do you view cooking? How do you see your role in cooking? If you say that you 'hate' cooking, or that you are a 'bad cook' or feel resentfully that it's 'your job', you end up subconsciously looking for clues to support what you think. Frustration can get amplified when it's time to cook. Your partner gets blamed quickly for not helping out. You lose patience and give up trying to foster inclusion before anyone really gets a chance to contribute.

All these things can be changed by simply reframing your beliefs. Change 'I *have* to cook' to 'I *get* to cook'. Remember that the way you describe yourself and your relationship to food passes directly on to your kids – so all change comes from you. It takes a little practice, but when you reframe how you see cooking, you will find your whole experience gets better, and it all becomes so much more *hyggeligt* (cosy). If you love cooking already, consider yourself lucky and make sure to share your passion!

Beliefs	Reframes
'Cooking is a chore.'	'Cooking is my choice.'
'I hate cooking and am terrible at it.'	'I enjoy cooking when I have a clear recipe to follow. I've made some delicious meals everyone loved.'
'Cooking is a woman's job.'	'In our family, everyone shares the task of cooking.'
'I usually make whatever is easy.'	'I take pride in making nutritious meals for my family whenever I can.'

Empathy

Let children overhear you complimenting each other. Danes are naturally gifted at pointing out the good and kindness in others due to their upbringing and education. It really makes an impression when you hear it. You might say, 'Aren't we lucky to have such a sweet mom/dad who is good at making food?'

The more you point out that you value cooking and helping each other, the more children will see and feel the value in it. Not everyone loves cooking, and that's fine – no need to force it ceaselessly. We can all help in different ways, but it is something we need to do to make our family run. You won't always have the time and energy to make the meal you wanted, and that's OK. Using the microwave or a frozen back-up plan is just fine. Kids love these meals too, and can also easily make them on their own when necessary. Go easy on yourself and remember the big picture. If you don't make a big deal out of it, it won't be a big deal.

No ultimatums

Children learn naturally by testing things out and making mistakes, and this is also true in cooking. As you observe your children in the kitchen, ask yourself, 'Am I fostering curiosity or correction? Am I being relaxed, or overly critical and vigilant?' It can happen that we can get scared because something crashes and we worry our children will hurt themselves. We yell, scold or blame as a knee-jerk reaction: 'Oh no! What did you do!?' This is usually just because we've had a shock. It isn't because we mean to blame them. No child wants to hurt themselves on purpose or spill or break something. If you do scream as a reaction, just make sure you apologise and let them know that accidents happen. Help them clean up. Repair and reflect, and then correct. You could say, 'Sorry I sounded upset! I know that was an accident. I was just scared. You were probably scared too. Are you OK? Let's clean this up together.' Be aware of your language and try to be prepared for spills, curiosity and exploration.

Togetherness and hygge

Any food that you can make and eat from the same pot or shared in the form of little bowls of food for everyone to enjoy is considered very *hyggeligt* in Denmark. Eating from the same place creates a feeling of shared cosiness. Here are some examples of 'hygge food' to cook and eat together:

- **Fondue:** Everyone dips their bread in cheese, or vegetables or meat in broth, or strawberries in chocolate. There are many variations.
- **Table-top grill:** Everyone cooks their own meat or vegetables to enjoy with a fondue or raclette.

- **Pizza:** Prepare the toppings together, make the dough, create your own pizzas and cook them one by one so everyone tastes each other's inventions – very *hyggeligt*!
- **Stews, pasta dishes and soups:** Choose big pot recipes everyone can eat from, with breads for dipping.

Cooking alone can also be super hygge. You won't always have the surplus energy needed to involve your child, and this is fine. Find a nice podcast you want to listen to or call a friend, have a glass of wine or a cup of tea, and immerse yourself in the meditative joys of providing nourishing food for your family. This time can be enjoyed as a choice and self-care, not a chore.

Cooking with toddlers (0–3)

Inclusion, curiosity and exposure to food

The Danish Way of cooking (like most activities) is all about inclusion. From early on, the objective is to be around cooking and food together, because it's this exposure that cultivates curiosity. Toddlers love to be with you, so letting them join you in the kitchen is the perfect way to foster a love of food. Remember:

- Take them seriously. They want to help.
- They don't want to be annoying.
- Cooking can be playful.

Things to keep in mind when cooking with toddlers

Your toddler will thrive on feeling part of the 'real deal' and pretending they are working with you and contributing to the meal. If you are going to try to involve your little one in the cooking process, it's important to bear a few things in mind:

- It will take a lot longer to complete things – and that's OK. Slow down and don't rush them.
- It will be messy – and that's OK. Respond to spills or mistakes neutrally – 'Whoops' – not critically –'Oh, not again!'
- Involve them in the clean-up process. Ask them, 'What can we do to clean that up? Let's do it together.'

Remember the acronym FAIL: first attempt in learning. Mistakes are absolutely part of the process

Find ways for your toddler to help

Look for areas in which your little one can help, and give them a task. For example, they might be able to:

- help you look for cookbooks
- hand you ingredients ('Can you pass me a carrot?')
- help you take things out of drawers
- take things out of low parts of the refrigerator
- clean up messes with you (have sponges and cloths on hand)

Your child might be too young for some cooking tasks, but they might be able to contribute by:

- breaking off beans or asparagus
- cleaning potatoes
- cutting soft things like cheeses, hot dogs or cucumber
- washing vegetables
- cracking an egg
- using a whisk
- pouring water into a mixture

Dealing with frustration

Remember that struggle is a part of learning. We want kids to be challenged, but not so much that they give up. This is called the 'zone of proximal development' or the 'sweet spot' of learning. So when your toddler feels frustrated because they've tried to do something and haven't been able to, wait until they are about to give up and then offer some assistance.

Show them: 'Would you like me to show you?'
Offer help: 'Would you like me to help you?'
Do it for them: 'Have you tried turning it? Here, we turn it like this.'

Sometimes they will refuse your help and their frustration can turn into anger. This is also part of their development, and they can try it again another time. Be patient. You can let them know you understand that they are annoyed: 'Oh, that was irritating!'

Symbolic tasks and parallel play

You can always give your toddler symbolic tasks to do along-side you so that they feel like they are part of the cooking experience. Here are some ideas:

- A wooden spoon and a pot to play with will be more than enough for a baby.
- Let them open and close Tupperware lids.
- Give them measuring spoons and cups, and some dry ingredients like flour.
- Pour dry pasta or beans into a colander or strainer for them to play with.

Involve the five senses?

Danes are very good at play and sensorial learning. Studies show that the more children experience food through the sens-es, the more willing they are to taste it. As much as you can, think about how to talk about the five senses while cooking, and try to give words to your toddler's experiences.

Touch: 'Is it mushy, squishy, soft?'
Smell: 'How does it smell? Does it smell good?'
Sight: 'What colour is it?' 'Is it red or green?'
Hear: 'It sounds crunchy.'
Taste: 'Does that taste yummy or sweet?'

Playing with water

All children love to play with water. If they can stand, try to let them clean pots or wash something in the sink. Playing with water while washing or exploring in a big bowl in the sink is a great way to have your little ones be present with you in the kitchen. They can also play with a sponge, squeezing water from one bowl to another. You could ask them:

'Let's see what happens if we pour the water from that cup
  to that bowl.'
'Is the water cold or warm?'

Give your child freedom to explore. They will probably get some water on the floor and on their clothes, but this is just part of their play. They will learn with time. If you put a towel down and have the mindset that it's no big deal, and it's natural that things might get a bit wet, you will have a much better time – and so will they.

Making potions

If you don't have enough time or energy to involve your little one in the cooking process, set up a bowl or a big cup for them to make a magic potion or mixture. Give them any extra stuff you have on hand and let them be creative. Kids can spend a long time mixing and stirring and playing with their magic potions while being together with you in the kitchen. Potions can be made with:

- rice
- pasta
- flour
- sugar
- milk
- water
- washing-up liquid

> ♪ **Reframing being 'a lone martyr' ♪**
> **to being 'a playmate'**
>
> My two-year old niece, Selma, was visiting us with her
> parents recently. She really wanted to play with me, but I had
> to cook dinner, so my default answer was: 'I can't play now,
> I have to cook.' I looked for a toy to give her something else
> to do. But then I reframed. 'Selma, do you want to help me
> cook?' Her eyes lit up and she nodded excitedly. We washed
> her hands and got her up on a stool next to me. I gave her
> some mozzarella pieces she could take apart and some basil
> she could rip up to put in the pasta salad. She was beaming
> with pride and was so happy to join in. It was funny to realise
> how my change in perspective meant we combined work
> with play and everyone was happy. Whether it's a real task or
> parallel play, togetherness is the goal.

Cooking with young children (4–6)

The benefits of cooking

Studies have shown that kids who learn to cook from an early
age have an advantage when it comes to language skills and
basic maths skills. In Denmark, cooking is seen as an absolutely
essential life skill and it's a big part of both school and *skolefrit-
idsordning* (also known as SFO), the 'free-time play school' where
almost all children go after school to play (and cook and bake).
It's also a big part of most children's home lives. Danish kids
learn to cook throughout their childhoods, and this helps them
with collaboration, self-confidence and self-esteem.

Mestring (coping)

Mestring is one of the hallmarks for what parents and schools want for kids. It basically means when you are able to manage or cope with something on your own. It could be tying your shoes, putting on and taking off your clothes, making your bed or cooking – it can be anything you 'can manage', and it's not typically tied to academic pursuits. We underestimate how much being able to cope with simple day-to-day tasks can boost a child's confidence. It is highly overlooked in many cultures. Danes tend to actively look for different areas of life in which to give their kids 'wins', because this sets them up for an 'I can' mentality in many other fields. It's quite impressive when you see it happen.

If you are just starting out, look for things in the kitchen that your child can do with minimal supervision and involvement from you. For example:

- mixing eggs
- tearing and rinsing lettuce
- stirring dressing or sauce
- sprinkling cheese on a finished pizza

Keeping kids sharp: working with knives

Danes seem to take a lot of pride in how handy their little ones are with sharp objects. In Denmark, most pre-schoolers are already using real knives, but it depends a lot on your child and their motor abilities and sense of responsibility. Cutting things really gives kids a sense of trust and competence – it is *mestring*! Here are some things to know:

- Use a real knife, not a fake one. In Denmark, they use something called a herb knife, but this can be a 'kid-friendly knife'. It should be child-sized with a handle they can grip without slipping.
- It's important to use a sharp knife because you can hurt yourself more with a blunt one.
- Teach your child which side of the knife cuts (the sharp one!). This can take a bit of time for kids to figure out.
- Give them easy things to cut once you are comfortable with them using the knife, such as cheese and cucumbers.
- Don't communicate anxiety; let them know you trust them. You should definitely supervise, but transmitting fear is transmitting danger.

🥾 See your child as a partner, not a pupil 🥾

This is probably one of the biggest ways in which the Danish Way is different to other ways of parenting. The goal is not about 'quizzing' your child to see if they know how to do something correctly or can provide the right answer (treating them as a pupil). It's about speaking to them as a partner and showing equal respect. It's a subtle difference that yields massive returns as they grow up. Ask for help in a real way, using the sort of tone you would use with a friend (even though you may already know the answer). It's a lot about them feeling taken seriously; this will build *mestring* and natural self-confidence. Ask them:

'Which ingredient comes first? The flour? OK, got it. Then what's second?'

'Ah, so we have to cut it? Do you mean we have to cut the ends off, like this?'

'Hmmmm, so we have the butter, the cheese ... I feel like we are missing something.' (Pause to consider; if they tell you the answer, don't praise them –because it's not a quiz.) 'Oh yes, the eggs. Thank you. Here, do you want to crack it?'

Get into the flow and enjoy the company

That's the magic. Kids couldn't care less if things come out burned or ugly or lumpy (as long as we don't care). Invite them to participate in whatever capacity they can. Get into the flow together.

Remember the difference between *for you* and *with you*

Since children innately want to please their parents and make them happy, if we constantly praise their work, it subtly becomes about them doing things *for* you (as your pupil) rather than *with* you (as your partner). It can be a really interesting challenge to become more aware of your language and find ways to communicate that you appreciate your children being *with* you rather than doing something *for* you.

Cooking with older children (7–10)

Share the cooking role

Model, model, model. If you want everyone to cook, everyone has to cook sometimes. This is why it's important to get partners involved. Ideally, most of the time you should try to share out the household tasks in a way that reflects who most enjoys doing what. Equality in a relationship does not mean doing tasks equally. It can mean equanimity, which is different. This is doing things in ways that you all agree are fair. For example, I prefer to do the laundry, while my husband prefers to do the cooking. I like to do the supermarket shopping, he would rather take out the trash. Your kids will also have their preferences, but try to involve them in all the everyday activities at least sometimes.

Find the approach that best suits your family

Just make sure everyone has a role to play – even if it's only a small role because they have homework or other activities. Include them so it's understood that the family is interdependent. A child in this age range might help out by:

- helping choose the meal plan
- coming shopping with you
- peeling the potatoes or cutting up vegetables
- setting the table
- clearing the table or doing dishes

Not everyone loves cooking, and that's OK

There is no guarantee that just because you cook together, your child will love cooking. Many people like different things and this is no different for kids. What they need to learn is that cooking is part of what it means to be in a family, and that we all help out sometimes in some way, shape or form. If they love cooking, great. Enjoy it!

Use cooking to boost maths skills

Cooking presents so many opportunities to naturally build maths skills, such as:

- measuring and weighing the ingredients
- doubling a recipe
- converting measurements

Master chefs

Aim to get your kids to a stage where they feel total mastery over a few dishes on their own. These can be very simple or more complicated, depending on their skill level. My son started out being in charge of making popcorn on the stove for movie nights, and it really gave him a feeling of accomplishment. I could see that core feeling of *mestring* or competence in his face every time he did it. We scaled it up every year to increase the foods he could manage to make on his own. Ideally, at this age, you want kids to feel totally comfortable making a few things by themselves, such as:

- popcorn
- pancakes or crêpes
- sandwiches
- toast
- porridge
- easy pasta dishes

Since Danish children learn cooking as a subject in school, they will often make something in class and then take the recipe home to make it for the family. This is part of *mestring*. Choose one of your child's favourite dishes and help them learn how to make it so they can do it on their own. It can be 'their' special creation to make sometimes, enabling them to experience how satisfying it is to help the family with cooking.

Cooking with tweens and teens (11–16)

Don't give up!

If you didn't start before now, don't worry. And don't give up; think about it in the long term. Being able to do some basic cooking is a really important life skill that will help your kids stay healthier.

Maddag

It's very common for teens to have an agreed-upon *maddag* or 'meal day' each week where they are responsible for making dinner for the family. They can do it on their own or ask you for help. If they ask for your help, the roles are reversed. Now you are the one who sets the table, does the dishes or helps out as they need it. If there are siblings who are not too small, this is a nice way for them to work together, both at the supermarket and in the kitchen. There is something incredibly joyful about seeing your children making a meal together.

Forpligtelsesfællesskab

Togetherness has two meanings in Danish. One can be the normal kind, which is a bit like hygge, because it's generally pleasant and we can be together easily (playing games, having cake, etc). And then there is *forpligtelsesfællesskab* – 'responsible togetherness' – which is when we have to make a bit of an effort to be part of a group. It's not just about what 'I' need, but what 'we' need. We never think of this as something we have to learn, but for Danes, it is an extremely important part of their upbringing. You may not want to collaborate or cook together, but this is all part of what we must learn if we are to be in a community or family.

Everyone in the family taking responsibility for some of the cooking is a great example of *forpligtelsesfællesskab*. If we teach our children that being part of the family is also about giving up a piece of ourselves for the whole, it becomes easier and easier in the long run.

This can be as much of a lesson for us as parents and role models as it is for our children. We can't expect them to naturally join in with the things we want them to do if we don't join in with things they like to do too. Get your partner on board and model, model, model responsible togetherness.

Make cooking part of their weekly agreements and tasks

If your teen is getting an allowance, cooking and cleaning or taking responsibility for a 'meal day' can be part of their plan. This doesn't mean you can't make exceptions when they have things to do, but a general expectation that they are part of the food process is a way for them to become adults who know how to take care of themselves.

Keep connecting through cooking

Parents don't need to disappear for tweens and teens to be independent. Keep the connection open for as long as you can by, for example, including them and their friends in cooking and activities around food on weekends. This is a good opportunity to get to know their friends as well. Here are some ideas:

- Make pizzas together
- Bake something
- Have a BBQ
- Prepare a picnic
- Make a fondue and hot plate for meat/vegetables

Meal boxes

An increasingly popular thing to do in Denmark is to order meal boxes that come with the recipes and ingredients, like Hello Fresh. You choose what you will cook and they deliver the box with everything you need inside. These boxes can vary in terms of difficulty, but it's an excellent way to involve kids (especially if you are starting late). The timing and steps are laid out clearly, which can help your teen with time management, and choosing which meals to order together means everyone has a say.

Reflection and discussion

Tweens and teens can teach us about many things, so take the opportunity to reflect on and discuss what you are eating and what you learn from cooking different meals. As you cook, or at the table, try discussing:

- new ingredients you haven't tried before
- the cultural background or stories around different foods
- challenges faced in the cooking process
- different cooking techniques you've learned
- funny stories shared from the kitchen
- the nutritional value of the different foods you're preparing and eating

Eating

Parenting pitfall:
Bringing food baggage to the table

I realised when my daughter was very young that I had some issues with my relationship to food. I knew it wasn't healthy and that I would surely pass it on if I didn't choose to actively be aware of it. I made a vow to stop controlling food, to stop moralising it or talking about diets. There seemed to be far less pressure around what children were eating or not eating in Denmark, and much more focus on the framework around mealtimes and the atmosphere or feeling of hygge around the table. I was fascinated by this: the idea that the feeling of togetherness could be just as important as the food itself.

The truth is, we all come to the table with some kind of baggage from our pasts around food. Where you grew up and how you grew up will have an enormous impact on what you carry in those bags. With all the ultra-processed foods, excessive diet culture, food moralisation and mixed messages from the media, our experiences around eating can vary wildly. Only when we are willing to unpack those bags and examine the contents – what we liked and didn't like about mealtime growing up – can we provide our children with the ingredients for a healthier life. That is, it isn't just about the quality of the food; it's also about the quality of the presence of the people around the table. The more we can enjoy food for what it is, rather than overcomplicating it or seeing it as something to fight over, the more we can instil a life-long love of one of the most enjoyable and necessary aspects of our lives – eating.

PARENT tips

Play

Playing with food is totally natural and normal for younger kids. Danes are very good at finding ways to make the eating experience pleasant, especially if you come to an impasse. You can try to play games like 'How big are you?' (see page 76) or 'Show me how strong you are' (see page 82).

Choice and playfulness help keep mealtimes more pleasant. Danish *smørrebrød* (the open-faced sandwich, see page 85) is a great way to give kids the feeling that they can choose what to eat. As they get older, meals like fondue, table grills or pizza-making offer a way to be creative and playful, as well as being a chance to include their friends.

Authenticity

Using food to numb out, punish or control diminishes contact with our gut feeling. Having a strong 'gut' feeling is what guides us on the right path in life, and an honest relationship to hunger and our bodies helps calibrate that inner compass with our own true north. Always check in with what you are communicating about eating, even when you think you are not communicating anything. Our kids pick up much more based on what we model in our relationship to food than what we say about it. What are you signalling with your behaviour and language? Are you being kind to yourself? Are you being kind to others? Try to unpack your own food baggage and be aware. It takes a lot of effort to prioritise the family's good experience over our own triggers, but often there is no better motivator for self-growth than knowing how much we can influence our kids. Have honest conversations about food and health as a family, and try to walk the walk.

Reframe

Avoid calling your child a 'picky eater'. This risks becoming a self-fulfilling prophecy. It's completely normal to go through phases when they don't want to eat anything but white pasta or chicken nuggets. Evolutionarily, toddlers were programmed to be picky because it protected them from eating something poisonous, and studies show that kids might need to try a new food up to fifteen times before they like it.

In addition, try not to moralise or demonise food. Focus on listening to your body with kindness and treating food with appreciation instead. In this way, you will help your children to do the same.

What you say	What your kids hear	How to reframe it
'Ugh, I feel gross – I ate too much chocolate.'	'It's wrong to eat chocolate.'	'That chocolate was delicious. I can feel I've had enough now.'

What you say	What your kids hear	How to reframe it
'I am so fat. I need to go on a diet.'	'Fat is wrong. Control is important.'	'I am so looking forward to going to the gym this week!'
'I wish I hadn't eaten so much. I feel horrible.'	'Food is bad. Eating is bad.'	'That salad is just what my body is craving.'

Empathy

The aim for Danes regarding empathy and eating is for kids to develop trust in their own senses and needs and tune in to their 'gut' feelings, which will be part of their inner compass to guide them later in life. We are all born with an innate ability to know when we are full. Little kids may eat a lot one day and very little the next day, but they won't starve themselves. When your child says they feel hungry or they don't like the taste of something, for example, don't override them.

Child: 'I'm hungry.'

Parent: 'You can't be hungry. You just ate!'

Child: 'I don't like it.'

Parent: 'You do like it – eat it.'

How would you feel if someone constantly told you how you actually felt, and that they knew better than you did whether you were hungry? When children's boundaries are respected, they learn that they can trust in what they sense and that it's OK to say 'no' when something doesn't feel right. This is a key foundation for building true self-esteem and self-worth. It doesn't mean that you have to become permissive and not have boundaries – not at all. It just means that children always have the right to their feelings, senses and needs within a framework. We can help them develop empathy by believing how they feel.

No ultimatums

If we obsess over how much kids eat, we create unnecessary conflict and power struggles. Aim to give them a sense of control over their food. Put a little of everything on their plate and let them eat as they wish. Eating can be a battleground, not just with your kids, but also with your partner if you don't understand each other's pasts and agree on your big lines of parenting. It's one of those areas where it helps enormously to speak about your upbringing and engrained beliefs. If you start to feel triggered at mealtimes, ask yourself: 'What is causing this?' Remember that if you make a big deal about food, it becomes a big deal. That's why it's so important to get on the same page with your partner. Sit down with your partner and discuss the following:

- What are our beliefs and values around eating?
- What did meals look like for you growing up?
- What were you allowed/not allowed to eat? Were your senses and needs respected?
- What can we agree on as the big lines of parenting for us around eating? (Consider what you think your child should eat, expectations around food and eating, how you will manage power struggles, what routines you might adopt, what you'll do if they don't eat, what you'll do around family, etc.)

Togetherness and hygge

Danes believe that the feeling of togetherness while eating is just as important as the food itself (possibly even more important!). Food situations should be nice and cosy above all else, not marked by tension and focused on the fact that your children *have* to eat. Make the dinner table a sacred place and a media-free zone – establishing this at an early age will make it natural for kids to continue in this vein as they get older.

At the heart of hygge is the feeling of comfort. So, the next time you are eating together, run through the hygge checklist:

- **Safe:** Does the family know what to expect, more or less, each time we eat?
- **Pleasurable:** Is there some nice food and a cosy atmosphere?
- **Harmonious:** Are we getting along and not arguing about rules or having power struggles?
- **Present:** Is all tech and media off, and am I being in the moment?
- **Grateful:** Am I feeling gratitude for the food, and spending this time together eating?

Eating with toddlers (0–3)

Making the eating experience predictable helps avoid conflict

The more predictable meals are for your toddler, the more you can avoid power struggles. This means making sure that things look more or less the same way every day, and happen in the same order, so they know what to expect. This doesn't mean you can't be spontaneous or change things around a little (there is no right or wrong), but a predictable meal experience helps *a lot*. Here are some ideas:

- **Make a set eating area:** Make sure there are no distractions – turn off TVs, screens and phones. Use child-friendly and colourful plates, cups and cutlery. This makes 'eating time' a little more special.
- **Involve them in the process:** Whenever they are able to, let them help you to set the table, get into their chair on their own or pour water into their cup. Danes love the Stokke chair for kids, because it grows with the child from babyhood all the way up to their teens.
- **Eat by themselves:** Let them eat independently as soon as they are able.
- **Play with food:** This is totally normal for babies and toddlers, especially when the food is new. It's how they learn. They will learn to use a spoon and fork sooner if they are allowed to play rather than being fed.
- **Let them taste new things:** Offer different foods and tastes as often as possible.

Play ideas for the table

Hvor stor er du? **(How big are you?)**	A game many Danes play with their little ones at the table is: 'How big are you?' You ask this, and the child throws their hands above their head and everyone says, 'So big!' This is a beloved game for babies and toddlers. Just try it and see. It lightens the mood and makes eating more fun.
Hvor er Mamma? **(Where's Mamma?)**	In this game, you say, 'Where's Mamma?', 'Where's Dadda?', 'Where is Sophia?' Then you point to the person you are looking for and you say, 'Yes! Here is Mamma.' 'There is Sophia!'

Det er mine (This/these are mine)	In this game, you pretend you are going to eat what is on their plate, using your hands or a spoon to pull some food to one side while saying, 'This is mine!' They will usually take it and eat it themselves. It's a cute game that takes the focus off food scrutiny and makes eating fun.

Respect your child's feelings

Danes generally believe that kids should have the right to decide:

- **Their own senses:** what tastes good and what doesn't, what smells nice and what doesn't, what feels hot and cold to them
- **Their own feelings:** happiness, anger, frustration, sadness, pain, desire
- **Their own needs:** hunger, thirst, closeness, distance

Respecting your child is a very important part of developing their 'gut' feeling. When we *tell* our kids that they are hungry when they aren't, we are essentially telling them that we distrust what they feel. We are saying that we know better. If we say they *must* eat even if they don't want to eat, or that they *will* like a food even if they *don't* like the food, we are teaching them that their senses and personal boundaries don't matter. It's subtle, but over time, this can have long-term consequences.

If we respect our children regarding their senses, feelings and needs, we help them trust in their gut feelings, so that they are better able to identify how they feel and what they want, and can respect their own personal boundaries. Later in life, when someone wants your child to do something that doesn't feel right for them (such as trying drugs or having sex, to name two extreme examples), they may not be able to say 'no' if they have been taught to override their gut feelings to please others. Learning to trust your gut (literally and figuratively) is crucial to developing a strong internal compass and a sense of self and self-worth.

You can still set boundaries

This does not mean that the Danish Way of parenting is permissive parenting – not at all. Kids absolutely need help with a framework around eating, but this can be done respectfully. You can decide when and what the family eats, but let your children decide *how much* they will eat. There are other ways you can set boundaries around mealtime while still respecting your children's feelings. For example, you might agree on the following family rule for mealtimes:

> 'We will eat together, and we will sit in our chairs while
>   we eat.'
> 'We can be playful, but we don't throw food.'
> 'We have boundaries around snacking or other sugar
>   intake that affects mood and hunger.'

Eating in public or with the wider family

A lot of us feel stress when we are with our children around our wider families or in public. We become hyper aware if our children are not behaving 'correctly' and eating the way we know our parents or other family members think they should. This stress we feel, consciously or not, automatically transfers on to our children and can actually ramp up food conflict.

PRE-FRAMING AND REFRAMING

To avoid this, you can use a technique called 'pre-framing', in which you visualise how you would like the visit to go. Set up the scene in your mind, and see what strategies you can use to stay out of conflict. The more you pre-frame ways to deal with things that normally annoy you, the better prepared you are to deal with them.

You can also use this opportunity to practise empathy and reframing. If you find yourself getting frustrated by your mother-in-law giving your child a treat that you hadn't planned for her to have, you might tell yourself: 'My mother-in-law likes to give her chocolate because she thinks that's what grandmas do. It's not to go against me.'

STAY TRUE TO YOUR VALUES AS A PARENT

If you catch yourself feeling overly critical of your child around others, remember that our kids are not an extension of our self-image. They are individual beings with their own senses, feelings and needs. Do they really need to clean their plate or eat their peas right now because Grandma thinks they should?

Express your boundaries

When you feel it's necessary, take the talks.

'I know you would like her to finish everything on her plate, but she ate enough and she knows when she's not hungry.'

'I'd prefer it if you didn't give him a juice now. Whenever he has a juice, it takes the edge off his hunger and then he eats less at dinner. He can definitely have one during snack time, though.'

Eating with young children (4–6)

Remember that snacking too much will throw off the dinner routine

The more you are able to have a set routine and schedule for eating, the easier it is to understand when kids are hungry. Aim to regulate snack time and dinnertime. Even a glass of juice can make a child feel quite full, if they get that in the period before dinner.

Behaviour is often tied to blood sugar

A child's reaction to food is often about how hungry they are. If they have eaten too much in the afternoon, then they probably won't be very hungry at dinnertime. Or if they haven't eaten enough, they may be so hungry that they need to regulate their blood sugar to feel better. Eating to regulate blood sugar will surely affect how they are acting. Using empathy will help you to understand where they are coming from and react accordingly. Being understanding rather than angry is a good place to start. Think about how you feel when you are over-hungry (or, indeed, too full) and go from there.

Don't get hung up on how much they are eating

You might feel that you would like your child to eat more, or you might be worried that they are not eating enough. Remember, a problem is only a problem if we make it a problem. Here are some things you can try.

- Make sure there is at least one thing on the table that your child likes, but always encourage them to taste all parts of the food.
- Don't study what they eat or don't eat.
- Cook for the whole family without paying special attention to the individual child, and try to involve them in the cooking.
- Let them take it at their own pace.

Dealing with picky eating

All kids pass through picky eating 'phases'. This is totally normal. Be careful not to fret and label them as 'picky eaters', as this can become a self-fulfilling prophecy.

What can make picky eating worse?	What can make picky eating better?
Restriction or punishment for not eating	Modelling good eating behaviour and not getting stressed about it
Rewarding with food or moralising food	Involving kids in food prep and cooking
Disapproval, blame or shame, including labelling them 'a picky eater'	Laying out different food options and encouraging them to try new things.
Snacking or having erratic meal times and experiences	Having a clear framework and consistent routine around eating

Eating holds no moral value

Saying things like, 'Good girl, well done for finishing your plate!' or 'Be a good boy and eat this, because Grandma made it,' teaches kids that eating holds some kind of moral value. How much you do or don't eat does not make you a good or a bad person.

Fifteenth time's the charm

As we saw on page 72, studies show that kids need to be exposed to new foods up to fifteen times before they get used to the taste – so just keep offering them whatever they claim they 'don't like'. Keep that statistic in mind. Don't force them to eat it, of course, but if you offer them the new food over and over again, very often they will eventually like it.

Give grazing options

In Denmark, they love to put out little bowls of different things to try for snacks and meals. It's shared food, which is hygge, and it also gives children the feeling of choice and being in control. Put out healthy choices, and you'll set up healthy habits. Here are some common Danish examples to put on the table, but you can be creative and try different things:

- carrots
- cucumbers
- cherry tomatoes
- cut-up cheese
- edamame beans

🥾 Old Danish game: 🥾
'Show me how strong you are'

After the age of about two, kids are aware of growing bigger, and this game taps in to that. It works surprisingly

---

well to encourage children to eat vegetables or something healthy. After they eat their broccoli, for example, you ask to feel their muscles and say, 'Wow, I can feel that!', suggesting that the broccoli has made their muscles grow. You will be surprised how many times they go back for more so you can check their muscles again. The message is always that good and healthy food makes you bigger and stronger.

Teaching manners

Many parents are worried about table manners, but don't stress about it too much. Just keep being clear and consistent with the messages and they will get it.

- Model good manners yourself.
- Use humour to correct and explain consistently. For example, if your child slams their spoon down, playfully cover your ears and say: 'Ouch! That hurt my ears when you put the spoon down. That's why we put it down softly.'
- Practise manners in non-pressurised environments, like role-playing being at a restaurant or having a tea party with dolls.
- Avoid correcting your child or making a scene out in public or with guests. This can feel degrading and humiliating (just as it would for you).

Having boundaries

Rather than forcing your child to do something, make it clear that there are boundaries around eating and build them into the framework of mealtimes. Boundaries can look like:

- 'This is what we are having for dinner. You can decide how much you eat.'
- 'I know you love chicken nuggets, but that is not on the menu today.'
- 'We don't take food to the sofa or away from the table.'
- 'When we sit at the table, we can join the table talk. Not when we go away.'

If you and your partner don't agree about the rules, don't discuss them at the table in front of your child. Talk about it later and adjust the boundaries for next time.

Eating with older children (7–10)

Eating together is important

In a Canadian study (the first of its kind), researchers followed children from the age of five months up to ten years to see what effect eating together had on them in the long term. Controlling for all other factors, the study found that children who ate with their families were more likely to show health and mental benefits many years later. By the age of ten years old, they had higher levels of fitness, lower soft-drink consumption and more social skills, and were less likely to self-report being physically aggressive, oppositional or delinquent.

No TV or screens at mealtimes

Screens can be distracting and defeat the purpose of hygge at a family dinner. An interesting fact from the long-term study was that if they had the TV on during family meals, it actually spoiled the effects. American kindergarteners who watched TV during dinnertimes were more likely to be overweight by the time they were in third grade. This association between TV and being overweight in children was also reported in Sweden, Finland and Portugal.

Simplify breakfast

The Danish love of minimalism seems to extend to food and eating. Oatmeal is the main staple of a Danish breakfast, served cold or hot with few variations. Having fewer choices – two, for example – generally makes mealtimes run more smoothly, because the framework is consistent from early on. But this means agreeing with your partner and saying, 'This is what we eat for breakfast.' You can come up with your own main options (toast, oatmeal, eggs – whatever is right for your family) but try to keep the choice limited and healthy. If unhealthy options are introduced in the week, it can be a struggle. At weekends, you can introduce different options.

A Danish classic: *smørrebrød*

Smørrebrød (pronounced 'smur brud') is a Danish meal staple. These open sandwiches are enjoyed almost every day in some families. S*mørrebrød* is so easy to make (you just put out different toppings and the bread base), and it's a great way to offer healthy options. Kids make the sandwich themselves at the table, which gives them that important feeling of autonomy. Any dark brown bread will work as a base (you generally eat *smørrebrød* with a knife and fork and cut it in half first), but if this feels too strange, you could just make sandwiches, starting out with any bread you like and a selection of toppings or fillings. Some of the options could be:

- hard-boiled eggs or egg salad
- pâté
- hummus
- tuna salad
- cucumber
- lettuce
- peppers
- tomatoes
- carrots
- pickles
- roast beef or different meats

Watch your weight talk

As I mentioned earlier, be aware of how you talk about yourself, your child and others regarding weight. They are listening to how we talk to them, but also how we talk to ourselves. Children may go through phases where they are bigger or skinnier, where they eat a lot or very little. This doesn't make them a good or bad person.

Try not to:

- comment on your own weight or put yourself down
- comment on others' weight

- comment on your child's weight
- demonise food
- label different foods as 'good', 'bad' or 'naughty'
- yo-yo diet or binge

Instead:

- aim to be a good role model for eating and exercise habits
- put out healthy meals and snack options
- don't restrict or force their eating – remember, they are in charge of their own feelings, senses and needs
- don't keep a lot of junk in the house – if it isn't there, it's not an option (that goes for us too!)

Eating with tweens and teens (11–16)

They will be *hungry*

As puberty kicks in, be ready with a lot of supplemental meals if you don't want your teens to snack on too much junk. Think nutrient-rich and positive calorie-dense. Every child is different, but be prepared! Some useful foods to have on hand include:

- cereal or oatmeal
- toast with avocado
- smoothies
- cheese tortillas
- hummus
- yogurt bowls with granola and berries

👢 Teens do want to talk! 👢
The truth about teens and dinners

In a recent survey, American teens were asked when they would most like to talk with their parents, and 'at dinnertime' was their top answer. Kids who eat dinner with their parents have less stress and a better relationship with their family, and are more likely to do well academically in school. There are so many proven benefits to eating together as a family that it's a wonder it isn't prescribed to parents for all ages of children.

Don't interrogate them with questions like: 'What did you do today?', 'What did you get on that test?' or 'Do you have homework?' Authentic communication means including yourself in conversations, not just interrogating. This opens up space for them to ask you questions as well. You might share something like: 'Today was tough for me. I had to make a deadline, but I managed.' Remember to communicate the feeling that you are a real person, not someone who is monitoring them.

The way to the heart is through the stomach

Most tweens and teens will have a favourite dish they have enjoyed throughout childhood. If they seem down, or if you just want to connect or express your love, try cooking their favourite meal. There is something very comforting about the sounds, smells and tastes of your favourite foods. This is usually appreciated.

Invite their friends to eat with you

The more you get to know your child's friends, the more you will stay connected to your tweens and teens. Eating together is an excellent way to do this. Whether it's a study date or a sleepover, make your table (and attitude) as open, welcoming and enjoyable as possible. It doesn't have to be formal, just pleasant and inviting. You'd be amazed how much you can learn at the table together. Danes say we have two ears and one mouth, so we should listen twice as much as we speak.

Create a 'going out to eat' ritual

Most kids will enjoy going out to eat. This doesn't have to mean going to a fancy restaurant. You can choose something that works with your budget and schedule, and whether it's once a week or once a month, try to create a special ritual – a breakfast, lunch or dinner out that you can look forward to. If sometimes they can't go, or don't want to, that's fine, too. Be flexible and don't take it personally.

Tweens and teens *do* eat more junk

It can be quite stressful for parents whose children have eaten more or less healthily all their lives to watch as their kids grow up and begin to snack on junk food and soda. But try to relax, because eating junk food is a part of teen life. Danish teens also eat a lot of junk. Rather than shaming or criticising them (or worrying), understand that this is probably a phase they need to go through. It's only a big deal if we make it a big deal. They will go through phases, and they are in charge of their bodies. Reframe and promote the positive storylines in their lives instead. For example:

- Focus on healthy habits like sports, exercise and adequate sleep.
- Be a good role model – this is super important! Talk the talk and walk the walk, and model the behaviour you would like to see.
- Focus on meaningful mealtimes being pleasant above all else.
- Keep healthy options you know they like in the house.
- Don't buy junk food unless it's for planned hygge moments or special occasions.

Respect your teen's time

Because they might have other things on – such as home-work or planned activities with friends – try to include them in the meal plan for the week, so they can tell you when they will be around. This way, they have agency and can feel like a part of the family's plan. If your teenager has made plans with a friend, for example, work around that, just like you would do with your partner. Be respectful and don't stress if your teen can't join you for a meal. Danish families are really good at working together and not stressing when kids can't come to dinner. There might also be occasions when your teen doesn't want to join you at the table – they may not be hungry, or they might be in need of time alone. As long as the framework and the values are there, you can be flexible. This is not to say that the family should always ad-just to suit the teenager; it's more about communicating and coordinating out of respect for each other's time and needs.

Remind them of mealtimes

An hour before eating, let your teens know that dinner will be ready in an hour. Repeat this half an hour before eating, and again a few minutes before. It helps the tween or teen to manage their time so they won't feel frustrated at being interrupted in the middle of their homework, phone call or computer game.

- **Name the time:** 'We are planning to eat at seven o'clock – I wanted to let you know so you can have that in mind when you are gaming with your friends this afternoon.'
- **Remind them:** 'Remember, we are eating in an hour.'
- **Final reminder:** 'Just so you know, we are eating in ten minutes.'

PART 2

ROUTINES

Having routines is one of the best ways to keep the big lines of parenting in place and avoid power struggles. Routines are especially beneficial for sensitive and strong-willed children because having predictability in their day-to-day lives helps them feel more secure and gives them room to negotiate within some clear, set boundaries. In Denmark, having routines is considered extremely important for a family's wellbeing. The family's routines are usually one of the first things that professionals will look to improve or strengthen if parents are struggling at home. The reality is, no one really likes to feel that their life is unpredictable and random. Having a familiar framework for what to expect every day helps reduce anxiety, creates more peace and opens up more opportunities to parent with respect.

Routines help to create connection in four key ways. They:

1. **Reduce power struggles:** If we don't have clear expectations, then it can become easier to skip things like toothbrushing or schoolwork, or to settle for a later bedtime. Alternatively, we may lose our tempers because we just want it done 'now!'. Having routines helps us send clear, consistent signals. When children know that 'this is just what we do, and this is when we do it', it is easier to lead with respect because expectations are understood. It also gives them some room to negotiate and feel in control of their choices.

2. **Help cooperation:** Routines help reduce stress. When kids know what comes next and they get a warning of it well in advance, they tend to feel calmer because life isn't happening randomly. They feel less bossed around, which means they're less likely to rebel. Many of us don't realise how quickly we slip into an angry and controlling tone.

3. **Foster independence and self-confidence:** When children learn to do things like brush their teeth, take a shower, set up their schoolwork or make their beds by themselves, it naturally instils a sense of mastery and independence. Not only does this make them feel competent, but it also builds self-esteem.

4. **Help us schedule in more special hygge time together:** Sometimes, as parents, we get into a habit of just rushing from one thing to the next, feeling flustered and overwhelmed rather than taking time to enjoy our children. Having a routine makes it easier to schedule in connection time. This can be things like a cuddle and a story before bed where we are really present, quality playtime with building blocks or art materials after dinner, or a planned baking activity at the weekend. These are all easier to manage when we have routines and know what to expect.

Mornings

Parenting pitfall: Believing I wasn't a 'morning person'

One thing I really didn't want to do as a parent was to boss everyone around in the mornings, full of stress. Despite my best intentions, however, I found myself running around, barking orders and dishing out ultimatums. Stress overtook me, and I morphed into the frazzled, angry mom I really did not want to be.

I knew that the Danish Way of reframing was based on the idea that all change starts with a change in language, so I started looking at my limiting beliefs. Something I repeated to myself incessantly was: 'I am just not a morning person.' Where did I even get that idea – and how true was it? Wasn't it also true for me to say: 'I love mornings with the kids when I get up earlier and prepare myself first'? Yes, it was.

So, I started repeating that mantra instead, and I planned for the mornings the night before rather than doing it all at the last minute. I worked on my sleep hygiene and made our morning routines a lot clearer. I practised pre-framing my green script the night before, asking myself how I wanted my morning with the kids to look and feel. I visualised it, and it had a tremendously positive effect. It may sound silly, but I tried to set my intention as soon as I woke up, telling myself: 'I am going to have a good day today.' I crawled into bed with the kids for snuggly wake-ups, hugs and cuddles as often as I could. I sang morning songs and tried to be more playful. I lit candles at the breakfast table to create more hygge, and was much more aware of seeing that morning time as sacred. It wasn't a magic wand; I didn't always have the patience, and occasionally morphed back into frazzled mommy. But I apologised when I needed to, and I was more honest when I was at my limits. I tried to go easier on myself rather than beating myself up. This simple act of self-compassion made me nicer to others. Waking up and changing my language was like opening a window on to the positivity and beauty that was available at the start of our days. It was always there – my words just made it easier to see.

PARENT tips

Play

Playfulness can be a good solution if your child is sad, tired or not cooperating in the mornings. It helps you have a better day, too. This is all about your attitude. Taking five minutes to physically connect in the morning makes a big difference, whether this is jumping into bed for a snuggle, doing 'This little piggy went to market' or singing a morning song to wake everyone up. A playful start will generally put everyone in a better mood. Use play to move kids along: 'Hurry up and finish getting dressed so we can do a puzzle before we go.' Try sarcasm and humour with your tween and teen (instead of nagging): 'I see the slug juice trailing behind you. What are the chances we are going to get out on time?'

Authenticity

The more honest you can be with yourself, the more genuinely you can show up for your kids in the morning. Ask yourself, how am I feeling? How much surplus energy do I have?

Being authentic doesn't mean yelling and screaming because you 'feel' like it, any more than it means plastering on a fake smile and using a perfectly happy tone while suppressing rage. It means deciphering what is really going on for you emotionally.

Our difficult feelings disappear much faster if we just acknowledge and accept them, rather than ignoring them. The key is to be curious about what we are feeling, and to give ourselves the same grace and compassion we would like to give our kids. You might be thinking, *My morning sucks and I feel helpless.* Try saying to yourself, 'I feel angry because I wanted this morning to go better. I feel like a bad mom – but I am not a bad mom. I am just having a bad day.' Remember that you can love being a parent and also have a terrible day of parenting – both things can be true.

Reframe

Don't label yourself or your child negatively. As I discovered for myself, if you say you aren't a 'morning person' or that you 'hate' mornings, you reinforce this belief. If you say, 'When I wake up earlier to get ready and have time for hygge and playfulness, I really enjoy the mornings,' you change your whole experience. Scientific research firmly backs this up. Our words have incredible power. Calling your child 'scatter-brained' or 'forgetful' when they can't find their shoes and bag can also influence their belief system. They may think, *If Mom and Dad say I am scatter-brained and forgetful, I must be.*

By simply changing your language to focus on the more positive details (and there always are positive details), you can build up that storyline instead. Remember that all behaviour has meaning behind it. Your tween may be undergoing massive brain changes. They could be tired or growing, which may cause them to be forgetful. Look for how you can be more supportive rather than shaming, blaming or criticising. Give them strategies like always putting their bag in the same place or making a list of what they need to take to school each day. Make a point of noticing when things go well, and the values you like in your child, so you constantly strengthen the positive storyline.

Empathy

What can you realistically expect from your child in relation to their morning routine? This will vary depending on their age and abilities. Are they independent? Do they need more time for getting dressed? All parents and kids will have some morning issues, no matter what. This is normal. Apologise if you have had a bad morning: 'Sorry about this morning. I was in a really bad mood. It wasn't your fault.' These moments of reflection and apology are where we create deep respect and connection with our kids (contrary to what many parents think). In Denmark they say, 'When your child behaves in a way that doesn't invite compassion or a hug, that's often exactly what they need.' This is true for all of us, from toddlers to teens to parents. It's good to remember that sometimes it is precisely during our most unreasonable, selfish and unlovable moments that we need to be loved the most.

No ultimatums

Choose your battles. Avoid nagging. Use humour. Kids feed off our energy, so work on your own stress, tone and vibe before you give them a message. Do you need to take five minutes to breathe or pass the baton to your partner? Try 'if, then' statements that lead to something playful or *hyggeligt*, rather than using threats or ultimatums. For example: '*If* you hurry up and get your shoes on, *then* I'll find your favourite song and we can listen to it in the car. I'll race you to the car.'

Prepare the night before. Have the morning routine start in the evening by laying out clothes and bags, and setting an intention for the next day. Make a list. Have a present moment with your child where you get down on their level, put your hands on their shoulders, look them in the eyes and give them the message. This will help reduce power struggles. When this doesn't work and your child refuses, be gentle but firm and stick to the plan. Give natural consequences. If they don't want to put on their coat, let them feel the cold. Know your boundaries. We can acknowledge our children's feelings, but they also need clarity. You can say: 'I know you want to get dressed by yourself, but now we need to go.'

Togetherness and hygge

There are so many ways to carve out time for hygge in the morning. This could be lighting candles at the breakfast table, or crawling under the covers and waking up your kids with cuddles. It could even be stopping somewhere for a hot chocolate before school, if time allows. Sometimes, teens will be more open to allowing you in and talking in the morning while they are getting ready. Take your coffee, and if there is an invitation into their world, take it! Hygge can come in many forms. The key is being aware so that you can spot opportunities for some 'we time'.

Mornings with toddlers (0–3)

Slow down the pace

Toddlers and young kids don't like to rush. Rushing can make them dig in their heels even more, meaning the morning routine takes twice as long. The more you can slow down, the smoother things will go.

Think 'independence age', *not* 'terrible twos'

In Danish, the toddler years are also referred to as *selvstændigheds-fasen* or 'the independence age', rather than 'the terrible twos'. It's completely normal for young kids to want independence, which usually manifests as them insisting '*I want to do it!*' Rather than seeing this behaviour as annoying and uncooperative, try to meet your child's natural developmental needs. This creates fewer power struggles, because you will meet them where they are at rather than putting negative labels on them.

Finding opportunities for independence

Make sure to carve out the time to let them learn to do things on their own. It's OK to help when they need it, but be patient! You may need to be a zen master to wait for them to put on their own clothes or shoes, but you will be rewarded with more time and a happier, more capable child in the long run. Avoid tight, restrictive clothes and anything with lots of buttons, laces or complicated buckles. Instead, buy clothes that make it easier for them to dress themselves, such as:

- shorts and trousers with elastic waistbands
- shirts with large openings for their heads
- shoes that fasten with Velcro

Let them put on their clothes and shoes themselves. Resist the urge to do it for them – instead, sit down, have a cup of tea or coffee, and breathe. If they get frustrated, help a little bit, but only enough to help them move forward with the process. This might look like opening a strap or holding a sleeve so they can get their arm in. Stand back and let them know that you're there to help if they need it.

Look for the meaning behind their behaviour

No one wants to be called annoying or to be accused of making you have a bad morning. We all have reasons for why we behave the way we do, and the Danish Way is based on trying very hard to get curious about what is actually happening for you and your child, by focusing on the meaning behind behaviour. So instead of saying:

'Oh, You are so grumpy!'
'Stop being so angry! We are going to be late again!'

Try:

'I can see that not being able to get your shoes on is really
    irritating for you. Let me help you.'
'I know that was hard. This was just a really dumb morning
    for both of us.' (This puts you on the same team.)

🥾 Choose your battles 🥾

A lot of kids go through phases where they want to decide
what to wear (or eat, sleep, say, etc), which may not be
exactly what you want. Remember, this is how they feel their
independence. They may want to wear clothes that completely
don't match, or Spider-Man pyjamas, or their favourite T-shirt
three days in a row. Ask yourself: does it really matter if they
wear that outfit one more time, or their clothes don't match?
Decide whether this is a battle worth fighting.

Give them choices

Giving your toddler choices helps them feel that they have a
say. For example:

'Do you want to get dressed now or after breakfast?'
'Do you want the red bowl or the blue bowl?'
'Would you like to wear this shirt or this one?'
'It's time to put your shoes on. Do you want to put them
    on, or do you want me to help?'

Know your boundaries and set limits

When you run out of time and really need to leave, just move
forward. You don't need to always 'convince' your child about

every boundary you set. Once you have asked them to do something (allowing time for them to process your request), be gentle but firm. You can acknowledge their feelings, but it may mean picking them up to leave, so they know you are consistent. You could say:

> 'You really wish you could stay at home, but now we have to go.'
>
> 'You really want to get dressed on your own, but it's time to leave. I am going to help you put the last things on.'
>
> 'I am not leaving without you. I'm putting on my jacket, and I'll be by the front door.' (Don't threaten to leave without them; you won't actually do so!)

Mornings with young children (4–6)

Prepare the night before

If you think about it, mornings can be a lot to deal with! We are jolted out of unconsciousness into wakefulness, and are immediately put under clear time pressure. We have to be organised while also needing to collaborate with little people who have underdeveloped executive functioning skills when it comes to things like focusing, planning, prioritising and self-regulating emotions. This is not easy! Starting the morning routine the night before can make a huge difference. Here are some ways you can prepare in advance:

- go to bed earlier (you and your child)
- check the weather forecast, and choose and lay out suitable clothes

- pack your bags and prepare lunches
- plan your morning intention (for example: 'I want some snuggle time and playfulness, and I don't want to be angry and rushed')
- plan what you will have for breakfast and how the choices will look

Read books about routines and transitions

Many Danes read a book series called *Lotte and Totte*. These books explain to toddlers and pre-schoolers the different routines they can expect in the mornings, along with every other 'routine' and transition you can think of. These kinds of books are very simple but effective and are so useful when you need to set the framework more clearly for the day ahead or help children deal with any transitions or challenges happening at home. Some example topics include:

morning routines
potty training
preparing to become a sibling
a new baby in the house

Another popular Danish kids' book, *Karius and Baktus*, teaches kids about toothbrushing (see page 142).

Use a routine chart or pictogram

This can be especially useful for children who struggle with executive functioning skills. Charts or pictograms help children see what they need to do next, which gives a sense of predictability and makes them feel safe.

Morning routine

Remember: keeping kids little isn't helping them

Many parents like to keep their kids 'little' for as long as possible. They teach them to cooperate by being helpless and dependent. Unfortunately, this is often more about the parent's needs and desires than it is about the child's. If you are tempted to continue putting on their shoes for them, dressing them, etc, try to see the world through their eyes. It can be really frustrating to have to wait at the kindergarten for help getting ready to go outside and play when they see other children getting ready on their own.

Setting up your home for self-reliance and hygge

If you want to save time looking for things in the morning and make it easier to have a clear routine, look for ways to organise your home so everything has a place – ideally where kids can reach them. This also keeps things feeling neat, cosy and hygge. Here are some ideas:

- hooks for hanging coats and scarves
- a place to sit to get shoes on and off
- a place for storing shoes
- a basket for gloves and hats

Getting out the door

Actually getting out the door in the morning can become a huge power struggle for many parents. Due to stress and time constraints, we fall into the habits from our own childhood of yelling and using ultimatums: 'If you don't come now, you are going to be in big trouble.'

While difficult, aim to be ready ten minutes before the planned time to leave. This builds in time for unexpected events like a sudden need for the bathroom or missing shoes.

Check your language and try changing ultimatums to 'if, then' statements that are positive and playful rather than threatening. By focusing on something positive or *hyggeligt*, you avoid threats and ultimatums and can change the whole mood. Play is key. Try saying something like, 'As soon as you are ready, I'll race you to the bus stop. Last one out is a rotten egg!'

Be curious and compassionate with your own feelings

Despite your best intentions, your mornings may not always go to plan. In these cases, it's important to meet yourself with compassion. The more you take your own situation into account, the easier it is to show up authentically for your child. It's OK to have a bad morning. This is normal and a part of life. Say to yourself:

- 'Oh, I can feel it's a stressful morning for me.'
- 'I am having a hard time. I can feel I don't have the patience I would like to have.'

Involve the teachers

Danish parents let teachers know whenever their child has had a difficult morning or is having a hard time in general. They might tell them in person during drop-off, or in a text or email. This is expected because it helps teachers be more empathetic with the child that day. Even if this isn't typically practised in your culture, try it. It makes a huge difference to your child's wellbeing when you act as a team with the school to scaffold them emotionally.

Mornings with older children (7–10)

Wake up earlier and get ready first

Some children really need more time in the morning for it to go smoothly, and this can dramatically reduce stress. Let's face it, we need more time too! Try to get up earlier so you can be more present. Ask yourself: 'What's my emotional intention for this morning?', and bear this in mind while doing the practical things. It's a cycle that comes back to you: stress begets stress, and calm begets calm.

Allow for autonomy

Independence looks different at different ages. Letting your child do things themselves doesn't mean you can't still help them, remind them, make breakfast and so on. Doing things *fælles* – as a joint family team – is very different to doing things 'for' your child. By now, they should be able to:

- wake up
- make their bed
- get dressed
- make breakfast
- brush their teeth and hair
- remember extra sports gear or instruments for school

Routines can change

Be flexible and curious. Psychologists have found that families who develop flexible routines that adapt to kids' developmental phases are less stressed. You still want to have a clear framework to be flexible within; boundaries are important.

For example, sometimes children really aren't hungry in the morning. This can be a phase. It's OK to occasionally let them not eat as much. If skipping breakfast becomes a thing, get curious about what could help. Ask yourself:

- Would it be nicer to sit together in the morning, and make breakfast a cosy family meal?
- Would different foods help? Could you offer some other (limited) options? (Remember, too much choice can create confusion – see page 85.)
- Could they take a snack to eat later if they really aren't hungry right now?
- Would it help to let them eat breakfast in front of the TV? Some kids don't feel 'social' in the morning and enjoy quiet time to wake up while they eat. My son had a phase like this. It didn't last for ever, but it helped for a period. He eventually returned to the table. You know your child best.

Have conversations

Talk about what is going on at school, finding out about what they're learning and what activities they're doing. When we know what is going on in their worlds, we can help them prepare and remember what books and other relevant things must be packed.

Keep messages simple

Even much older children, including teens, can have a hard time understanding several messages at once. This has to do with executive skills functioning; it has nothing to do with their academic level. It's very different from child to child (and adult to adult). We may feel like they are ignoring us when we ask them to do things, but they may just need more time to process the information. Here are some tips:

- **Discuss the morning routine the night before:** Ask your child, 'What are the main things to remember for school tomorrow?' This shouldn't be a quiz, just a gentle reminder.
- **Give one message at a time, and wait ten seconds:** After you have asked them something, e.g. 'Do you have your notebook?', count (in your head) to ten before repeating it so they have time to process.
- **Try a routine list:** If mornings are often a struggle, use a morning chart or checklist.

🥾 Make it a treat 🥾

They say seventy-five per cent of the time you'll get to spend with your kids is over by the time they turn twelve. Family dynamics change significantly after that. At some point, the morning routine will become considerably easier: wake-up times, breakfasts, packing bags and getting out the door should all be pretty rote. So, whenever you can, make it a treat. For example:

- Put a nice note in their lunch box telling them you love them.
- Surprise them with their favourite breakfast.
- Let them sleep in. Have a nice morning together and take them in late.
- Have a surprise special day. Do something cosy together when they're not expecting it, like going to the zoo, visiting the beach, or enjoying a special lunch date. It's a good investment in the memory bank.

Mornings with tweens and teenagers (11–16)

Promote healthy sleep

Missing sleep has a tremendous effect on all of us. It's important to be aware of the need for a consistent sleep schedule, so this is something to discuss regularly with your teen. Inconsistent sleep can cause drowsiness, memory loss and cognitive issues, along with irritability and mood swings. If your teenager is struggling with not enough (or poor-quality) sleep, talk to them about:

- stopping caffeine earlier in the day
- not eating too late
- using an app to track the quality of their sleep
- turning off screens an hour before bed
- not dramatically shifting their sleep schedule at the weekend
- trying a sleep mask and ear plugs

The ideas above are as important for us as they are for teenagers – and teens don't like hypocrisy. If you talk the talk, make sure to walk the walk.

Build systems to create good habits

Just because your kids are older and can do things by themselves doesn't mean they won't forget. Everyone is different. Some kids will be able to manage completely on their own, but many will still struggle with executive functioning skills. Just like for adults, having systems to help them build good habits is really helpful. Encourage your teen to:

- prepare bags and clothes for the next day in the evening
- keep their keys, money, wallets or cards in the same place so they always know where they are
- hang up a weekly schedule so everyone can see it
- help them put together a checklist of what they have on that day and what is needed
- give time checks in the morning

Reframe: it's biology, not laziness

The more we understand this and reframe, the more we can have empathy and help support our teens rather than judge them and feel frustrated. It can feel very comforting when parents help teens find their missing things. It doesn't mean taking over and doing everything for them while they lounge on the sofa, but they are not being forgetful because they are careless.

Avoid nagging

Why? Because it's annoying. Nagging can also increase a child's dependence on you, which Danish parents don't want. Help them take charge of their own lives, support them when necessary and encourage them to take responsibility without nagging them. This can take practice. You might say things like:

> 'I can see that you are running late and have a lot to do. Should I get the computer for you?'
> 'You can't find the book? Do you remember where you were sitting and reading yesterday?'

Don't say 'I told you so'

Sometimes we all suffer the natural consequences and unpleasantness of being late or forgetting something we really needed. No one – not teens, nor adults – wants to hear 'I told you so'. You can empathise with your child by saying, 'That sucks,' or 'I hate it when that happens.' You can help them find solutions. but being righteous doesn't generally go down too well.

Problem-solve together

Getting teens out of the house in the morning can take teamwork. Instead of fighting about punctuality, brainstorm solutions during low-stress times like the weekend. Remember to get ideas from them so you can make a plan that will work for everyone.

Afternoons

Parenting pitfall:
Missing the most important meeting of the day

There was a period where I really took for granted meeting the kids after school. When I picked them up, I would be on a call that I felt I just couldn't finish. They'd run out to me with arms outstretched, artwork in hand and stories to tell, only to be shushed so I could keep talking. I was in my own world and merely a driver to the next item on the to-do list. I am not proud of this and feel bad even writing about it. When I saw signs up in Danish schools that depicted a phone with a red line through it and saying: 'Get off your phone, you are about to have the most important meeting of the day,' it really struck me. Danes put a lot of importance on how you greet your child after school or when you come home from work. I had completely lost the plot.

I started to make a concerted effort to put my work away before I picked them up in the afternoons. If I came home later than them, I took some time to meditate on my green script in the car to mentally prepare myself for some genuinely tuned-in playtime. I turned off my phone and made sure I gave long hugs whenever I saw those little faces. We scheduled in more hygge time in the afternoons, and once a week went for ice cream. I learned so much about their days in those moments. Work and the to-do list were always waiting for me, but time passes in an instant, and I knew my kids wouldn't always be waiting for me. It's hard to parent the way we would like to all the time. This is normal. But we can always ask ourselves: 'What is the most important meeting I have today?'

PARENT tips

Play

Play is the way that many kids unpack their days, which helps them have less baggage in the future. There are entire schools dedicated to free play in Denmark, and almost all Danish children attend these schools in the afternoons. There is a deep belief that kids need unstructured free play in their days. Make 'play' stations in your home for little kids that you can rotate through: an art area, blocks and construction, sensory toys and pillows, play kitchen, a door swing. Take a nature walk. If you are too exhausted to engage much with your child, try the ten-minute rule. This means giving your child your *full* attention for ten minutes of play and togetherness. If you fully devote those ten minutes to them (no phone or work), it will help free you up to do what you need to do afterwards: 'Now, you can keep playing blocks while I start dinner.' For older kids, sports, dance, music and more organised activities are common play activities, but they will still greatly benefit from non-adult-led unstructured play and downtime.

Authenticity

In Denmark, they don't say, 'What you don't know won't hurt you,' but 'What kids don't know hurts them.' In other words, it's important to be honest in an age-appropriate way. Having difficult times is just part of life and not something to hide. If we want our kids to be honest with us, we need to model honesty. If you consider that children are brilliant at reading our inner states, then it's only respectful to tell them the truth. Being honest doesn't mean giving overwhelming details about our day or putting unnecessary stress on them (absolutely not). It's about letting them into our emotional lives in an age-appropriate way. For example, you might say:

> 'Can you see I'm not so fun to play with today? It's because I had a bad day at work. It has nothing to do with you!'
> 'Oh no, did I forget to listen to you? I'm sorry. It's just because I've been really busy at work and I started thinking about it when we were playing. Can you explain it again?'
> 'Do I seem angry? Oh, it's so good you told me! I'm not angry – or, at least, I'm not angry at you!'

Honesty also helps prevent kids from filling in what we don't say with negative thoughts – something most people (adults included) have a tendency to do. If our partner is ignoring us, for example, we may assume we have done something wrong rather than thinking it's a work problem. This is why it's so important to respect how clever our children are. Never underestimate the power of authenticity. Don't give complicated details, just be honest. We can't always be in a good mood, any more than they can! This kind of honest relationship will mean a lot in their teen years.

Reframe

Danish health authorities advise parents to be really aware of speaking positively about others (other parents, other kids, their teachers, the school) because we are what they call 'the invisible classmate'. This means that whatever parents say to their children comes into the classroom with them. If we judge others, our children will do the same. If we look for the good in others, our children will do the same. If we take conflict in a healthy way, our children will do the same.

We can indirectly affect our child's wellbeing and that of the class by being better at reframing at home. Ask yourself: 'Am I being a good role model when I talk about others?'

Instead of saying, 'Oh, I can't stand that parent,' you could say, 'I don't always agree with that parent, but she is super helpful with the PTA.' We don't help our kids with their relationships by using negative labels like 'He's mean,' or 'She's a bully' or 'I hate her.'

When we look for the good in others, and forgive their mistakes, our children know that we will forgive them when *they* make mistakes. Taking this approach helps your child become better at understanding others, dealing with conflict in a healthy way and focusing on a more positive storyline.

Empathy

It is important that we are able to handle our children's feelings without judgement, and that they feel safe sharing their feelings with us. There are no good or bad emotions, there are just emotions. With smaller kids, a good activity is to draw your mood together after school and talk about it. This gives a snapshot into their feelings that day, and is a great way to foster conversation. As they get older, they may come to you for advice about issues with friends. Aim to be their safe space and give them the time they need to share what they're feeling. If your child has a bad day and seems to take it out on you, try not to take it personally. This takes tremendous energy on our part as parents, and we won't always have that. If you experience a rupture with your tween or teen, don't hold a grudge. You are the adult, and you must model maturity. Remember: they need you. Keep coming back over and over for positive connections – a smile, a hug, kind actions. Experts believe it takes at least five positive interactions to every negative one to keep a relationship strong.

No ultimatums

Predictability in the afternoons will help avoid power struggles. Simplicity and routine are highly encouraged by the Danish health authorities, because it is believed that the more time you are able to spend with children in the early years, the less conflict you will have in the later years. As they get older, don't have rules just for the sake of having rules. Try to listen and be flexible and find solutions together. You might say, 'I can hear you really want to go out with your friends. I am just concerned about you getting your work done.' Be clear about what you do and don't want, and remember that if you have been flexible and trusting with your child, it's likely your teen will be flexible with you. If you establish a democratic style of communicating, they are more likely to listen to you. Don't make 'no' your typical starting point.

Togetherness and hygge

Schedule hygge into the afternoon routine. Whether it's going for a hot chocolate, an ice cream or a leisurely walk, make cosy time together a part of your everyday afternoon routine. The key to hygge, however, is not just the activity, it's the feeling. One way to bring your emotional green script into focus is to make a mental note of glimmers (nice things about your child and the moment) rather than triggers (stimuli that evoke negative emotions). Looking out for these glimmers can really help you get into the hygge space. Pay attention to:

- the way the light shines on their face
- the cute or funny way they say certain things
- their pride in showing you something they have made or done
- the sound of their laughter
- how it feels to hold them
- how much they have grown
- how much you love them

Paying attention to these glimmers can remind you of how fleeting and precious time is. Breathe in the moment.

Afternoons with toddlers (0–3)

Be wary of falling back on screentime

Feeling insecure about routines can lead to more screentime. If you find yourself wondering, *Should I play with my child, or take them for a walk outside, or have a snack, or take a nap?*, it can make the default answer handing them an iPad. It's harder for parents to have clear boundaries when the daily structure is too loose. Building a routine means you know what to do and when, which helps everyone feel secure and reduces power struggles. You can build the framework just the way you want it.

Predictability makes kids calmer

Having a clear framework also creates a sense of peace. If the blue script (what is going to happen) is clear for everyone, then the green script (how we want to feel during the happenings) becomes much easier to work on. Try to see life through your toddler's eyes: 'When I come home, I know what to expect. We take off our shoes and I play with my dad. This is how it is. I can count on this.'

Make a routine that works for you. It might look something like this:

- take off jackets and shoes at the door
- wash hands
- have a snack
- enjoy hygge time – read, play, snuggle, watch something
- take a nap

Let them sleep outside

Put your child outside for their afternoon nap as often as possible. Danish babies are left to sleep outdoors every day, even in very cold weather (obviously wrapped up warm!). It's believed that the fresh air and natural noises help them sleep better and cry less. Interestingly enough, according to a study of different nationalities, Danish babies cry less than babies in other countries. A combination of calm and consistent routines and fresh air seem to make an enormous difference. If you live in the city, you can dress them in warm clothes and let them sleep near the window.

Remember that everyday activities are play

Toddlers like to help. They will naturally want to join in. Work is play for them. You need to have the patience and energy, but the earlier they take part in household tasks, the more you are guaranteed to have a helper in the house later on. You can spend some time in the afternoons:

- tidying up together
- organising cushions
- doing laundry

See pages 21–2 for more ways to include your toddler in household chores.

Afternoons with young children (4–6)

Greeting your children after school

As we discussed on page 114, picking up your kids from school is the most important meeting of your day. It's the first time you will see each other after a long day, so make the effort to show them you are 100 per cent there for them so they genuinely feel you want to see them. Don't underestimate this moment of re-establishing connection! Here are some tips.

🥾 Danish recommendations for making it 🥾 a 'good pick-up'

- **Turn off your phone:** Keep your phone turned off or put it on silent, and put it away for a while.
- **Make physical contact:** Greet your child with hugs and kisses. Wait until your child pulls away from the hug.
- **Make eye contact:** Show them that you are genuinely interested in *seeing* them by making eye contact as you greet them.
- **Stay with them in their physical space:** Stay close until you feel you have made a warm connection

---

Step inside the school

Danish teachers encourage parents to come inside the classroom and see what their child is doing once a week, rather than always waiting outside or in the car. Instead of saying, 'OK, I'm here, let's go!', take a look at what your child has been doing. If they are drawing or doing something creative when you arrive, sit down and join in. Show them that you have time to be a part of the place and feel the atmosphere. Not every school will allow this, but if it's possible to make this gesture even once a month, it will mean a lot to your child.

Making small talk

Young children are living in the here and now. It can be difficult for them to respond to questions like, 'What did you do today?', because they genuinely can't remember. Instead of asking open questions, try finding concrete clues from the day to help guide them. You might just make an observation, rather than asking a question. If they aren't in the mood to chat, respect that without feeling offended. Just like us, children sometimes need quiet time after a busy day.

For example, if it's been snowing and you want to know whether they played in the snow, you might say: 'Wow, there's a lot of snow on the playground.' Then pause – this is important to give them time to reflect on whatever comes to their minds. You might then continue, 'I see you have your red mittens. Did you use those in the snow?'

A picture speaks a thousand words

It can be really helpful to see what has happened at school so you get clues to unlock your child's memory bank for conversations. All Danish schools and kindergartens have something called Aula, which is an online portal that parents are part of. Here, teachers post pictures that show what went on during the day. If your kindergarten or school doesn't do this, you could still ask for an email or message with some updates from time to time. This really helps spark meaningful 'small talk' after school.

Prepare the framework for your chosen routines

On the way home, it's a good idea to start talking about what will happen in the afternoon and evening, for example: 'When we get home, we'll take off our jackets and hang them up, then take off our shoes and put away your bag. Then we can wash our hands and have a snack.'

Afternoon snacks

Keep snacks simple. Less choice means more predictability. It's also important to regulate your child's blood sugar, which helps with mood and conflict. Be mindful of dinner, so don't snack on something too big. Here are some afternoon snack ideas:

- piece of fruit
- raisins
- yogurt
- bun with dark chocolate
- carrots

Hygge not homework

Danish kids don't get homework until they are much older, because Danes believe small children should be focused on hygge and play. This can come in many different forms, but it is absolutely a part of the routine. Here are some ideas for afternoon hygge:

- take a leisurely walk
- go to the playground
- go to the library
- have an ice cream
- share a hot chocolate and talk about the day
- play, bake or do chores together

Draw your mood

A wonderful way to get insight into your child's emotional world is through art. Ask them to draw their mood today or put their feelings on the face of a sun. This can give you a snapshot into their feelings and open things up for discussion. Many Danish teachers use this as a way to 'take the child's happiness temperature'. You can draw your mood, too, so it's a joint activity. Remember that all emotions are OK – there are no good or bad emotions, just emotions, so there is no need for judgement. It's about normalising expressing our feelings so your child knows they can talk about anything with you, and art can help with that.

Afternoons with older children (7–10)

How do you talk about others?

This period of your child's life offers an important opportunity for helping develop their empathetic language and ability to reframe. Danes do this more naturally because of their upbringing and education, but we can do it too with some awareness. Afternoons are a great time to hone these skills, because many of us have time to chat after school or on the way home.

Here are some recommendations from the Danish Health Authority:

Say hello to everyone	Make sure to say hello to both children and adults at drop-off and pick-up, and get to know their friends' names.

Be a good role model	Speak nicely about other children, parents, carers and teachers. Our kids mirror us. If we show openness to those who are different to us and speak positively, our children will do the same.
Ask if your child is upset about something	Acknowledge their feelings, but also remember that there are always more sides to the same story. Try to be curious about what happened from different perspectives.
Help your child think about different perspectives	Regarding conflict, help them think about whether other children could have experienced things in a different way, and how to talk about it with them if necessary. Speak with other parents or teachers before reacting to a conflict. Seek first to understand and then to be understood.
Invite other parents for coffee	Parents are highly encouraged to meet up with other parents – especially if their kids are having conflict. The belief is that it's difficult to talk badly about people you have met with. This has a tremendously helpful effect for the children involved and the entire class.

THE FUNDAMENTAL ATTRIBUTION ERROR AND REFRAMING

There is a phenomenon which basically means that we have the tendency as humans to look for good reasons for our own behaviour but blame others for theirs. We might think, *I was grumpy today because I didn't get much sleep and had a fight with my partner. She was grumpy because she's a jerk.* This is just a blind spot we all have, so being aware of it can help us become better at fixing it. Remember that using empathy to understand others, rather than using labels, ultimately makes us feel better too.

Thus, if you hear your child is having a conflict at school, try to help them separate the person from the negative label rather than just agreeing with them. You are the adult, and in the Danish approach, adults have a responsibility to help children use more empathetic language. Remember, there are no bad children. There are always reasons for behaviour. If we hold on to the good in people and separate actions from the person, we teach our kids that we forgive them when they act out or make mistakes. When we use more nuanced language, avoid black-and-white language, and look for the good in others, it helps our children do the same.

Here's an example of how this kind of conversation could go:

Parent: Hey, you had art today – how was it?

Child: It wasn't fun because Ryan was so annoying.

Parent: That doesn't sound nice. Normally you two are a good team. What was different today?

Child: He is just really mean lately. I can't stand him. He has been annoying for so long.

Parent: Hmm, do you have any idea what's going on with him? Didn't you tell me the other day that something happened with his parents?

Child: *(pause)* Oh yeah. He said they had a fight, and he had never seen his parents so mad at each other before.

Parent: Do you think that might be the reason? Maybe he is upset.

Child: *(reflects)* Yeah, I guess so. It could be that. I just don't like it when he acts that way.

Parent: No, of course. I understand it was annoying for you, and I know you usually love art. So did you get to paint at all?

Child: Oh yeah, I painted a really cool bird . . .

As the conversation continues, the parent could enquire and build up the positive storyline about painting the bird. They have subtly explored why Ryan might have been acting out without calling Ryan names or negating their child's feelings.

REMEMBER, RELATIONSHIPS CHANGE

We often side with our kids because we want to help them. But if we talk badly about others and label them as 'annoying', 'mean' or as 'a troublemaker', or if we say, 'I don't like him,' or 'Stay away from her,' it can actually make it more difficult for our kids to manage their friendships. If the relationship later changes for the better – as they often do – your child may feel they can't tell you and might hide their friendship. By fostering a more empathetic, less shaming style, you are helping your children grow up to be less judgemental of others – and you – in the long run.

Afternoons with tweens and teens (11–16)

Strategies for conversation

The time after school, as many parents know, can be a golden hour for bonding and communication with teens and tweens, but these conversations can also be tricky. Here are some general rules of thumb:

- **Avoid only asking about grades, test scores or accomplishments:** You want them to know you care about more than just achievements. Focus on what they learned rather than the end result. Instead of saying, 'What grade did you get?' try 'Did you learn anything interesting?'
- **Praise effort as well as achievement:** 'I am really proud of how hard you studied. I know it wasn't easy, but you stuck with it.'
- **Silence can be golden:** Read their mood and don't take it personally if they don't want to talk.
- **Ask questions that are non-judgemental:** 'Who did you sit with at lunch today?' or 'What did you eat?' rather than 'Why did you wear that?' or 'Why did you say that?'

A framework of trust

Routines become more of a flexible framework at this age in Denmark – and it's a framework based on trust. Routines are still important, but there will be a lot more activities and responsibilities and shifting timetables. Your relationship will matter now in a whole new way. Professionals in Denmark say, 'You can parent your child until they are ten or twelve, and then you can lean back and see the results.' If you are starting late, it's not too late, but your parenting must be done with respect for the person they are becoming, not who you want or expect them to be.

FOCUS ON TRUST, NOT CONTROL

Seeing friends after school is considered an important and healthy part of teenage life. It's good to have basic rules, but if your teen would like to stay later at someone's house in the week because they are watching a movie or playing a game, be flexible and aim for trust over control.

COMPROMISE

Don't have rules just for the sake of having rules. Listen to your teen and find solutions together. You might say, 'I can hear that you really want to go to this movie. I am worried about you getting enough sleep. Can you start it a little earlier?' Aim to find a solution in the middle. You still know better as the parent, but if you establish a democratic style of communicating, your tween or teen is much more likely to listen to you.

BE CLEAR ABOUT WHAT YOU WANT

If you really don't want your teen or tween to do something, be very clear about it. It's fine to say you don't want them to stay out, but be firm. If you have been flexible and trusting with them, then it's much more likely that your teen will be flexible with you. Just don't make 'no' your typical starting point or knee-jerk reaction.

As they close their door, keep your emotional door open

A lot of parents have a hard time when their children become pre-teens and teens because they no longer need us in the same way. When kids come into puberty, they need more physical and emotional privacy, and close their doors more often, both literally and emotionally. The key is not to bang on their door demanding more information, but to leave your emotional door open and check in more often.

Don't take their reactions personally – and always come back

It is *completely* normal that at this age, teens might not want to speak to their parents, and they might push back or seem to reject us. In the same way that it was healthy for the toddler to push boundaries, it's also perfectly healthy for tweens and teens to be able to detach from us. This is how they gradually build up a stronger sense of self and learn to manage more on their own. As parents, we will feel triggered and we won't always like these changes, but don't take it personally. If they don't want to talk, take it up again later – but *always* come back so they know you are here for them no matter what.

♫ Things to remember when you feel triggered ♫

- You are the adult.
- You must be the bigger person and model maturity.
- Show them you love them no matter what.
- Don't hold grudges or stay offended.
- Keep coming back, even when it's hard.

Make deposits in their emotional bank accounts

Remember, it takes five positive interactions to balance out every negative one. When you spend time with your teen or tween, try these ways to make deposits in their emotional bank account:

- **Give a smile:** Smile with your eyes, not just your mouth.
- **Give a hug:** Make some physical contact when you can.
- **Show kindness and respect in your behaviour and actions:** Even if you don't feel like it, these gestures matter. Do something nice for them with no strings attached.
- **Show interest in their hobbies or activities:** This includes screens – perhaps you can show an interest in a TV show or computer game they enjoy.
- **Create special moments:** Bring them their favourite snack or smoothie, or prepare a nice meal.
- **Validate their experiences and emotions:** Use phrases like: 'That must have been hard,' 'You must be tired,' and 'I'm sorry you feel that way.'

If they share something uncomfortable, remember that it's not about you

If your tween or teen tells you something upsetting – or you find out something upsetting – your job (ironically) is not to be upset. No matter what you are talking about, you can process how you feel about it later. It's easy to react if you don't like or agree with something, but try to remember: it's not about you. If you want them to come to you and be honest, they need a safe space. Here are some tips for what to do if your teen shares something you aren't comfortable with:

- **Be grateful they are sharing with you:** The fact that your teen feels they can talk to you in an honest way is hugely reassuring for both of you – so pat yourself on the back and feel gratitude!
- **Resist the urge to show too much emotion:** Try not to show that you're upset, shocked or offended.
- **Resist the urge to judge:** Don't say, 'I told you not to do that!' or 'How could you be so stupid?' If you do lose control and react, remember that no one listens when they feel upset or under attack, so just wait or connect before you continue the conversation. Say, 'I love you. I'm sorry for reacting so strongly. Thanks for telling me.' Give them a hug.
- **Manage your own anxiety about the issue:** Don't take it personally or berate yourself.
- **Don't jump in with advice and solutions:** Give them time to vent and think of solutions on their own. They may ask your opinion, which will be far more influential than telling them what to do unrequested.
- **Don't pretend it didn't happen:** Some parents prefer the 'head in the sand' response, but this is basically discounting your teen's experience. If they shared something with you or you have discovered something and they know you have, it's meaningful. Don't ignore it. Be curious and stay open. Pretending it didn't happen won't make it go away, but it may make them go away and feel ignored.

Evenings

Parenting pitfall:
Prioritising 'me time' not 'we time'

In the evenings, I had the habit of needing 'me time'. I would go into my room or disappear into my work and feel frustrated by interruptions from the kids. I didn't realise how antisocial I was being, nor did I understand that shutting myself off in the evenings was eliminating our opportunities for cosy time together with the family. I think we really value our individuality in this way in America. When I saw how common it was in Denmark to spend hygge time together in the evenings as a kind of daily routine, I started making more of an effort to be present. We would create an inviting atmosphere by lighting candles, brewing some tea and setting out evening snacks, and the kids naturally wanted to join. As they got older, we could also do our work in the living room together. Sometimes we would choose to watch a show or series, which was also *hyggeligt* and something funny we looked forward to. I could see how much the kids enjoyed it. By getting out of my comfort zone and practising giving up the 'me' for the 'we', I was also modelling what I would like for them. It is so much more natural for my children to stay in the living room together and spend evening hygge time of their own volition now than it ever was for me, which means it works!

PARENT tips

Play

Just as it is in the morning, play can be a really helpful way to lower resistance during the evening. The key is to have a few games and playful language ideas in your mental toolkit – things like saying, 'Here comes the pyjama police,' or suggesting, 'You can brush my teeth and I'll brush yours – let's take turns.'

Remember to give kids plenty of warning if they will need to stop playing in order to have dinner, and give them time to finish up so that what they are doing isn't brusquely interrupted: 'I know you are enjoying playing, but we are going to eat soon. Finish building that tower, and then we will eat.' Use the same approach with kids playing video games as they get older. Respect their play, and give them fair warning: 'We are going to eat soon, so please wrap up that game in ten minutes.'

Authenticity

Are you using language that expresses what you need and want in a clear and personal way? Using personal language means including yourself in the message. Sometimes parents get so focused on what they want their child to do that they forget to include their own needs. Always focusing on your child keeps you at a distance, and it can be disconnecting. So when you ask your child to put on their pyjamas and go to bed, you could also mention what your needs are, for

example: 'I'm sorry, but we'll only have time for one story tonight because I have to finish some work before bed.
Tomorrow we'll have more time.'

Watching movies or series together in the evenings can be
a good opportunity to have honest discussions about different topics like technology, sex, bullying or anything else that
comes up in the show that may be difficult for you to broach
normally. Don't be afraid to jump in and start these conversations when the topics come up.

Reframe

Your routines were going so smoothly, and then suddenly your
child started having meltdowns over toothbrushing, potty
training or bathtime – or they've become a rude teenager
seemingly overnight and you feel like all has been lost. Instead
of beating yourself up as a bad parent, or trying to 'fix' your
child, remember that these challenges are not a 'problem' –
they are a completely normal part of a healthy family life.
When we focus too much on a 'problem' and pay attention to
what our child can't or won't do, they can develop a real sense
that *they* are a problem, and this amplifies what's wrong rather
than what's right. Take a step back, get perspective, and focus
on the bigger picture.

It's totally normal to have fluctuations in the developmental process. There will always be two steps forward and one
step back.

Empathy

When you feel frustrated, don't speed up – slow down. Count
to five and breathe.

If you have more than one child, try to find a special time with each child on as many days as you can. This could be things like reading together, playing, or keeping them company in a bath or shower (if they still want that). Baths release oxytocin, inducing feelings of calmness and trust. It's important for your kids to feel like they can count on you. Being available in this way gives older children a chance to talk about difficult issues if they need to.

No ultimatums

We, as parents, have more power than our children. Therefore, we must take responsibility for *how* we use that power. This is the crux of equal dignity. The person with the most power is always the one who must try to improve the communication issues. Try to avoid 'I win/you lose' scenarios. Here are some ways to do this:

- **Offer choices:** 'Do you want to brush your teeth before, during or after the bath?'
- **Be collaborative:** 'Can you help me with this? Come on, let's do it together.'
- **Make it playful:** 'I'll race you! Let's see who is fastest!'

Many parents fall into the classic trap of being too diplomatic and not clear enough about what we are actually asking. We might try to be so nice and empathetic that we don't set clear boundaries. This can backfire, because kids don't understand what we really mean, so they don't do what we were hoping they would. Then we end up getting upset and becoming over-controlling, essentially doing exactly what we want to avoid!

Togetherness and hygge

Evening hygge time is very common in Denmark, and it's a wonderful tradition to adopt into evening routines for all ages. It's a way to invite tweens and teens to be part of the family without too much pressure. If you start this young, it becomes more and more natural for older kids to join in of their own volition. Try to devote some of your evening to being present with family. Of course, we have to be flexible, as there will be busier times than others, but parents set the tone. Hygge isn't just about what it looks like but what it *feels* like. It isn't demanded, expected or something kids are pressured into 'participating' in. Instead, it's a warm space to be drawn into – a place they are *attracted to*. Thus, our mood and the welcoming feeling contributes greatly. If you are new to this, just get started and keep doing it. If it's cosy, they will come. Common psychological attributes of hygge are feelings of:

- safety (a safe space)
- pleasure (yummy food and drinks)
- calm (no judgements or controversial topics)
- harmony (no competition, complaining, nagging or bragging)
- comfort (a place to relax)
- shelter (an oasis from the everyday where you feel part of your family)

Evenings with toddlers (0–3)

Build a simple routine

Whether it's morning, afternoon, evening or night, routines give a clear framework and predictability to your child's daily life. This can be especially calming for some kids, and helps reduce power struggles. Just remember to keep the message simple. Try to state what will happen in short sequential order without overcomplicating the message; for example, wash hands, eat dinner, play, brush teeth, have a bath, use the toilet, put on pyjamas, story and bed. As with breakfast routines, you may find a pictogram useful, particularly if your child struggles with distraction: see the example overleaf.

Winding down

Having a wind-down period is *so* important. This can include taking a bath, getting into pyjamas, and enjoying some quiet play and a story. Every family is different, and your wind-down routine may be unique to you, but try to keep it consistent and predictable. Sometimes we parents need a wind-down period before the children's wind-down period, to ensure that we can be fully present for them. Take a moment for a little meditation, for example, on how you want the bedtime 'green script' to go – this can help a lot. A cuddle on the sofa with your child can go a long way towards reminding you both what's really important, helping you connect to them and to yourself.

Evening routine

Look for 'win/win' rather than power struggles in the evenings

Transitioning from playtime to dinnertime, or bathtime or tooth-brushing can be challenging. Offering choices rather than giving orders and ultimatums can be really helpful, as we've discussed. You can also use these opportunities to give your toddler a sense of mastery. Ask them: 'Do you remember what we need to do now? Yes, we put pyjamas on. Can you show me how you do it?'

Bathroom set-up

Like other parts of the house, making the bathroom simple and functional helps foster more independence. Here are some things to include in your bathroom to help your toddler enjoy their bedtime routine.

- stepping stool
- toothbrush and toothpaste within reach
- soap they can use
- a low hook for their own towel
- a hamper or basket for dirty or wet clothes
- potty for potty training

Baths and hygge

If you have a bathtub, use it! For some children, baths can be sleep-inducing, while others get revived. Find out if baths calm your child and, if so, a bath can be a wonderful evening ritual. Here are some ways to make the bath extra *hyggeligt*:

- put lots of bubbles in

- have some bath toys handy and be ready to play
- don't worry too much about the splashing
- sing songs together
- have big, fluffy towels or robes for cosy dry-offs and cuddles

Toothbrushing

Toothbrushing can be a breeze for some families or a major struggle for others – and everything in between. If your child is resistant to toothbrushing, try to introduce an element of choice by having two toothbrushes, so you can ask, 'Do you want to use the red one or the blue one tonight?'

You can also avoid power struggles around toothbrushing through play. Here are some games to try.

Copycat	Brush your teeth together looking in the mirror so that they can copy you, but let them try to do it by themselves.
Sing a toothbrushing song	Make up a song to a tune like 'Wheels on the Bus'. For example: 'This is the way we brush our teeth, brush our teeth, brush our teeth.' Singing is so popular in Denmark, and any time you can make a song, you add fun and playfulness to your daily routines.
Be a food investigator	Say, 'OK, now I am going to check for any food that is hiding.' Begin brushing their teeth, but continue the game. 'Oh, I see a tiny piece of macaroni in there, I am going to get that!'
Make funny noises	Make animal noises like lion roars to encourage them to open their mouth. Just keep it short and fun. They will get it.
Pretend you don't know what the toothbrush is for	'Do I brush my nose with this? I forgot how to do it. Can you show me?'

KARIUS AND BAKTUS: THE DANISH BOOK THAT GETS KIDS TO BRUSH THEIR TEETH!

We read this book from when our kids were small, and it worked so well. It's a story about two 'tooth trolls', Karius and Baktus (playing on the words for cavities and bacteria), who have a good life living in the cavities of a boy who eats sugary foods and doesn't brush his teeth – but their homes get ruined when he visits the dentist and starts taking care of his teeth. If you can find a similar book, try it. These stories can be very motivating.

Evenings with young children (4–6)

Be clear about timings

People of all ages generally like to know when it's time to eat. In Denmark, kindergarten teachers give the kids plenty of advance warning and preparation when it's almost time to eat or change activities. This tends to help reduce conflicts.

'Now it is ten minutes until we eat.'
'Now it is five minutes until we eat.'
'Now it is time. Let's go and wash our hands.'

Don't be *too* diplomatic

Many parents try to be so nice and empathetic that we don't set clear boundaries or make it clear what we are actually asking our kids to do, which can mean they don't understand what we mean at first. Rather than being a gentle way to get them to cooperate, it can end up starting a conflict. Here's an example:

Parent: 'Don't you think it's about time for bed?'

Child: 'No, I want to play.'

Parent: 'But it's getting late. Aren't you tired?'

Child: 'No, I don't want to go to bed.'

Parent: 'OK, shall we say you can go to bed in ten minutes, after you brush your teeth first?'

Child: 'No! I want to play. I am not tired.'

Parent: 'Would you please be a good boy now and get ready for bed?'

Child: 'No! I don't want to go to stupid bed.'

Parent: 'OK, that's it! Now you go to bed, or you're not getting a story tonight! You never listen!'

WHAT HAPPENED HERE?

The mother starts with a rhetorical question and her tone is very soft: 'Don't you think it's about time to go to bed?' She is hoping her son will read the subtle message of what she wants, but kids aren't good at picking up on subtle messages. They need clarity. Her son takes control of the conversation, and then she ends up losing her temper (and her power) and becomes dictatorial. She blames him for the miscommunication.

'I WIN/YOU LOSE' MEANS WE BOTH LOSE

Remember that resorting to ultimatums and threats to 'win' what we want very often makes us lose. In the above example, the parent threatens to take away story time, which is an extremely important time of the day for emotional connection between her and her child.

GOOD THINGS TO REMEMBER WHEN COMMUNICATING WHAT YOU WANT

- Avoid rhetorical questions if you want to be very clear. Don't say, 'Isn't it about time for bed?' if you mean 'It's time to go to bed.'
- Don't say 'maybe later' if you mean 'now'.
- Don't say 'Would you mind . . .?' if you mean 'I want you to . . .'.

INCLUDE YOURSELF IN THE COMMUNICATION

When we include ourselves, we help our kids understand that we also have needs. This helps build trust because they know that we are being true to ourselves as a real person and not just playing the 'parent role'. For example:

Parent: 'Please change into your pyjamas and brush your teeth.'

Child: 'No! I want to play.'

Parent: 'I can see you are having a nice time playing, but it's time for bed now and I have to do some work tonight.

You can play for ten more minutes, and then we'll choose a story.'

Child: 'OK.'

Evenings with older children (7–10)

It's all in the routine

Routines remain important as children get older. An evening routine for a child in this age group might look like this:

- dinner (everyone clears the table and helps)
- homework (if not done in the afternoon)
- play a game
- TV or screentime
- shower
- brush teeth
- set out clothes for tomorrow
- pack bag for the morning

Support them in the process

As kids get older, they learn self-care and can bathe and brush their teeth on their own since we have helped them develop the habit, but it's still helpful to support them through the process. You could say things like:

'Are you getting ready for your shower?'
'How's it going in there? Soon I won't be able to breathe because of all that steam!'

'Hurry up and finish your shower so we can have some
cosy time before bed.'

Homework

Generally, Danes have a more relaxed view on homework
until children are older; younger ones are mainly just encouraged to read. Growing research shows that assigning hours of
homework to younger children has very little benefit for them.
However, children in most cultures do get homework early on,
so here are some Danish recommendations.

MAKING HOMEWORK AGREEMENTS

When making homework agreements, choose a time of low
stress so you are on the same page. Saying 'we can do it as it
comes' doesn't work for a lot of kids. You have to know your
child so you can help them find the right strategy. Once you
have agreed a strategy, your child will have a framework for
when, how and where to do their homework.

- **Agree on a specific start time:** Choose the time
  that suits them best. It might be as soon as they get
  home, or after a break, or after dinner.
- **Create a calm, dedicated space:** No phone, noise
  or distractions. Some kids benefit from you sitting near
  them while they work.
- **Offer guidance, not solutions:** Discuss strategies
  and problem-solving if they ask for help. Don't just give
  the answers.
- **Encourage self-checking:** Ask them, 'What other
  strategies have been working for you?'

- **Praise the progress:** Keep the praise on their efforts rather than innate abilities like being 'smart'. Focusing too much on being smart or talented has been shown to lead kids to give up more easily when something is hard because they are afraid to lose their 'smart' status. It's the perseverance and effort, not the 'innate talent' that matters most in the long run. Tell them, 'I like the way you figured that out. You didn't give up!'

🥿 Spørg igen, spørg en ven, spørg en voksen: 🥿 'ask again, ask a friend, ask an adult'

The next time you are about to give your child the answer to a homework question, consider the above sign found in many Danish classrooms. It means:

1. Ask yourself again.
2. Ask a friend for help.
3. If the first two didn't work, ask an adult for help.

This is very different from other cultures, where people often believe it's cheating to ask a friend for help rather than speaking to the teacher or an adult. However, this method:

- **Encourages independence:** They learn to figure things out on their own rather than defaulting to an adult.
- **Fosters collaboration:** Kids learn the same things in school and they are often much better at helping each other than their parents.
- **Helps them retain more information:** Studies show you learn more when you have to teach information to

---

someone else than learning it alone, so when kids ask
each other for help with their work, they are reinforcing
what they've learned.

- **Builds empathy:** Explaining something to someone
  else helps you to understand how the other person is
  receiving the information, which builds empathy.

Packing a bag for the morning means less baggage the next day

Getting into the habit of setting out clothes and preparing their
bag for the next day makes mornings easier. It's also good practice
because it helps them mentally prepare for the next day. Your
child can ask themselves, 'Do I need a change of clothes or shoes
for sports? Do I need to take any particular books or homework?'

If your child often discovers in the evenings that they have
forgotten to do something they needed to do earlier, it might
be a good idea to revisit your afternoon routines to make sure
they check in on what they need to do a little earlier.

Evenings with tweens and teens (11–16)

Chores

Many parents think that their tweens and teens are too busy
with schoolwork to burden them with any chores, and they don't
want to bother them by asking them to help with any duties. This
sounds loving and sensible, but it's not very helpful for them in the
long term. As we discussed on pages 15–16, we don't want kids

to assume that the home is a hotel and all services are provid-ed for them. This is part of what it means to raise an adult. It doesn't mean they have to do chores every day, but it's important for everyone to contribute. They will sometimes get annoyed at being asked to help (they are teens, after all!) but in Denmark it isn't considered a favour to always give them a pass from helping.

Hygge rituals

Evening hygge time is very common in Denmark. After din-ner, many families put on a pot of tea or coffee (this can be decaffeinated) and have a small snack – something baked, a piece of chocolate or some fruit – and read, play games or work together on computers in the living room. It's a way to invite tweens and teens to be part of the family without too much pressure. If you start this young, it becomes more and more natural for older kids to continue to enjoy evening hygge and join in of their own volition. Make your living room feel cosy and calm with some relaxing music and gentle lighting.

KEEP INVITING THEM TO JOIN HYGGE, BUT DON'T BE OFFENDED IF THEY SAY NO

Many teens want to be in their rooms or with friends, so it's good to go with the flow. Remember to keep inviting them to join you so they know you value them and would like their com-pany, but let them know it's also OK if they don't want to. A lot of parents feel hurt or offended when teens distance themselves, but it's natural for them to want more time to themselves at this age and it's no big deal. If they say no, let them know it's fine. Keep asking. Keep showing up. They will say 'yes' sometimes, and it will mean so much more when they do.

Bedtime

Parenting pitfall:
Communicating like a broken lighthouse

It was the end of the day and time to put my son to bed. I was totally exhausted. I had some work emails I needed to finish, and I was generally irritated and not in the mood to do the bedtime routine. My son was not cooperating at all. He wanted to watch a show and was refusing to budge, and I wasn't exactly being the person I would want to cosy up in bed with. My tone was bossy. I was barking ultimatums. Then, out of guilt, I started bargaining nicely and overcompensating insecurely. I gently pleaded with him. I was about to throw up my hands in despair and start yelling again when suddenly, I heard how I sounded. I was sending completely mixed signals. I took a deep breath. 'I am the parent,' I reminded myself. 'I set the direction.' I firmly and confidently told him he could have ten more minutes to finish his show – I could understand he wanted to finish it – but then he needed to come and help me choose a book. I then took five minutes and sat quietly alone in my room and meditated on my green script and how I wanted the bedtime routine to go.

I thought about how fast time passes, and how I no longer had these special nights with my older daughter any more. I promised myself I would dedicate the next forty-five minutes to him and not think about all my work stuff. I gave him a piggyback ride to bed, and we goofed around. Then we read from one of our favourite poetry books while we cuddled. He kept whispering, 'I love you, Mommy.' He was happy I was there and not 'the mad mommy'. This made me smile because I realised how tuned in to me he was. I was still very tired when I left his room, and my work was still there waiting for me, but I actually got energy from regrouping and making a conscious choice to keep my directional sense and priorities straight for what really mattered to me: hygge at bedtime.

In Denmark, parents are seen as a sort of lighthouse. They absolutely do not want their kids to fear them, but instead to respect them. This respect is won by sending clear and consistent signals, not using threats and ultimatums. We can let kids have a say in deciding what is going to happen before bedtime – which book to read, for example – but the direction should always be clear for everyone: 'I want you to go to bed now.' After all, a lighthouse is only effective if it is clear and consistent.

PARENT tips

Play

Make the bedtime routine and transition playful. Race them to bed. Be the tickle monster. Give them a piggyback ride. Role-play with stuffed animals. Sing together! The benefits of joint singing are enormous. Recite some nursery rhymes, with hand gestures to go with them, or touch and play with sensory books while reading. Play 'This little piggy went to market', or make shadow puppets on the wall. If we can make the bedtime routine playful in a way where we can genuinely let go and be silly ourselves, it makes the transition so much easier.

Authenticity

Look for books to read together that cover all topics and emotions, in an age-appropriate way. Bedtime is an excellent opportunity to have authentic conversations that span through life. Choosing a wide range of books and stories will help open this up. It's incredibly connecting to read about all aspects of life with children, and it is also scientifically proven to foster empathy and increase happiness in a 'count your blessings' kind of way. Remember, we don't need to have all the answers for our kids. We just need to be curious together, and honest about the fact that life isn't a fairy tale, and that's OK. This approach sets them up for more resilience and improved wellbeing.

If you have tweens and teens, try to be a good sleep role model for them. Staying up all night for work, watching Netflix until late, or helping your child with homework until midnight isn't sending the right message. When you make sleep a priority and show that you believe it's part of living a healthy lifestyle, children tend to follow suit.

Reframing

Meditate on the philosophical concept of 'the last time'. This reminds us that there will be a last time for everything. A last time you brush your child's hair or give them a bath. A last time you give them a piggyback ride. A last time they sleep in your bed, and a last time you will put them to bed. We never know when the 'last time' of anything will be, but when we focus on this, it can help us to put things in perspective and muster the presence to 'be there' for bedtime rather than in our emails or phone or daily stressors. It's a bittersweet exercise to think about the last time, but it is enormously helpful in reframing and getting present in our 'green script'. Make an effort to focus on what went right today with your child before going to bed, rather than what went wrong (as many of us tend to do by default). Go through the day, from morning to night, and think about any positive details you can remember. This is like a little mental treasure hunt; it strengthens the positive story in our own minds.

Empathy

Don't veto your children's feelings. Telling them they need to go to bed because 'Actually, yes, you *are* tired' is overriding how they may be feeling. We can't really know how our child feels, and telling them we do won't help them learn to trust themselves. Instead, try saying, 'I understand you don't feel tired, but this is when we go to bed.' This is respecting their senses while still being the leader. If they are acting out, ask yourself if there is anything they may be going through which could be affecting their behaviour. Has something changed at school or with friends? Is there anything going on in the family they could be sensing? Could they be ill or overtired? Try to meet them where they are with curiosity and understanding. They very often need extra connection and patience in these times, not less.

No ultimatums

Remember that you are the lighthouse. You set the direction. Your tone and non-verbal messages are just as important as your words. Good questions to ask yourself are:

'Am I being clear on the signals I am sending?'
'Do I sound consistent and sure of what I want?'
'Am I reflecting this through my language and tone?'

Many parents struggle with power battles before bedtime, so pay extra attention to anything that triggers you or your child and has a tendency to escalate, like stopping playing or watching a screen. Make extra time so you aren't rushing and there is less stress. Offer 'win/win' choices, rather than 'win/lose' ultimatums:

'It's time to wind down for bed. Shall we choose a book now or after we put your pyjamas on?'
'In ten minutes, we are going to start the bedtime routine. You want thirty minutes? OK, let's agree on fifteen so you have some extra time.'
'I want you to go to bed now, as we agreed. Hop on and I'll give you a piggyback ride.'

Togetherness and hygge

Make the bed really comfy with stuffed animals, blankets, pillows and nice lighting. Bedtime can be one of the cosiest times of the day to be with our children. Some children benefit from soft music or white noise. Others enjoy a massage on their feet or hands, or like to cuddle up and read with you. Try to make it cosy mentally as well. When kids feel we have the time for them, when we create that calm psychological oasis, it feels safe and special for everyone. These are opportunities to be with our children that will pass sooner than we realise; before we know it, they will be too big for this kind of hygge any more.

How much sleep does my child need?

Here are some recommendations from the Danish National Health Authority for how much sleep kids need.

Child's age	Hours of sleep	Sleep pattern example
1–4 weeks	15–18 hours	Small periods of wakefulness. Feeds every 1–3 hours throughout the day.
1–6 months	14–15 hours	Longest sleeping period 3–4 hours (few children sleep 5 hours in a row).
7–12 months	14–15 hours	70–80 per cent sleep through the night (i.e. at least 5 hours in total). There are two periods of sleep per day. The sleep cycle lasts about 50 minutes (growing to about 90 minutes).
1–3 years	12–14 hours	Most children now sleep through, sleeping about 5 hours straight at night, with naps in the day.
4–6 years	10–12 hours	10–12 hours at night
7–12 years	9–10 hours	9–10 hours at night
13–18 years	8–10 hours	8–10 hours at night

Bedtime with toddlers (0–3)

Give them choices

Giving your toddler choices at bedtime helps them to engage with their bedtime routine. They could choose:

- which book to read or song to sing
- how they want to get to bed (make it playful)
- which stuffed animal to bring to bed

Sensory books

Little kids generally love sensory books where they can touch and feel things like fur, rubber or scratchy materials that make noises. You can also look at the pictures in the book and talk about what you see.

Be consistent

Think about the lighthouse analogy I shared on page 152. Imagine you are a ship in the night. You depend on the light-house for guidance. Suddenly, the signal becomes very strong (controlling). Then it becomes very weak (permissive), changes direction (insecure), or disappears altogether (gives in). Would you feel trust in that signal?

The point is that sometimes, in our desire to be respectful, our leadership signals can get shaky and weak. We question ourselves because we want to be nice, but while children know what they *want*, they don't always know what they *need*, so it's up to us as parents to ensure they get what they need.

Kids are very astute and can sense if we believe in our own directions or not. Be consistent, and use personal language (for example, say 'I want you to . . .' not 'It would be nice if you . . .'). Be clear; be the lighthouse. And remember that it's not just about what you say. The tone you use, your body language and any 'in-between' messages you are sending will be seen very clearly by your children.

Singing before bed

Singing while reading stories or poems that rhyme is a very popular wind-down routine in Denmark, and something parents continue to do with kids for many years. Singing together releases oxytocin and endorphins, improves mood and even boosts immune function. Research also shows that singing and rhyming develops children's language skills and speaking ability, which makes it easier for them to learn to read later on. There are lots of song books in Danish that are used both for storytelling and songs. Try to find nursery rhyme books in your own language, or just sing together without books.

Staying up later won't help

Some parents think that if their child stays up later, it will help them sleep better, but in fact it typically winds them up. Staying up later releases cortisol and adrenaline, and can make it harder for kids to fall asleep and stay asleep. Be aware of their signs of fatigue and understand that most kids get tired at certain times every day; try to take advantage of that.

All toddlers need sleep

They don't all know it, and some kids are naturally better sleepers than others. It can be very difficult for parents who work late to give their children an early bedtime, but it does mean a lot for the child if you can. If you can't get them an early bedtime, try to make sure they get a nap during the day.

Co-sleeping

Many Danish parents co-sleep. If you choose to sleep in the same bed, just make sure there is no crack they can fall into, no big duvets and no pets in the bed. The Danish Health Authority recommends that the safest place for a small child to sleep is in their own bed in the same room as the parents. Some people have their child's bed at the foot of their own bed, others next to it. Avoid blankets they can get tangled in.

🧦 You know your child best 🧦

The Danish Way is not a strict formula with rigid sleep rules to adhere to. The most important goal is that parents feel as calm as possible when handling their baby. Nurses tell parents in Denmark that they know their child best, and that whatever works best for them is the approach they should use.

If your child is having trouble falling asleep or waking up in the night, here are some things to consider:

• Do you have an established bedtime routine?

- Do they have a clean nappy and enough to eat and drink?
- Are you irritated or stressed? Kids are very tuned in to us and they may struggle to sleep if our mood is tense. Pass the baton to your partner if you can.
- Have they had too many stimuli during the day?
- Have you been absent during the day? Some children can be restless when going to sleep in this case.

Baby and toddler wake-ups

When babies and toddlers wake up and signal for you, they benefit from a sensitive response, for example:

- Feeding, cuddling or rocking them back to sleep.
- Hold your hand around the baby's head, comforting them with your presence.
- Gently rub their forehead or the bridge of their nose.
- Sing a little song or talk in a low, soothing voice.

There are many ideas for what you can do; the key is to do whatever makes *you* the calmest.

Get support

All parents across the globe – and Danish parents are no exception – will experience some difficulties getting their child to sleep, and everyone in the family is affected by lack of sleep. On average, babies cry for a few hours each day – but some don't cry much at all, and some will cry more. You are not a bad parent because you find it difficult to cope with life with little sleep, and the best thing to do is to admit this and ask for some help from grandparents, friends or your partner so you can get some rest yourself. Staying up for hours on end with a child who can't calm down and sleep is stressful. Danes talk to their children, even as babies, to let them know what's happening. For example, they might say, 'I need to breathe for a moment, but I will be back in a little while.'

If you have concerns about your child's crying, it's good to speak to your doctor. Sleep problems and excessive crying can be signs that something is wrong.

Bedtime with young children (4–6)

Make sure you have the energy to focus on the bedtime routine

Can you be fully present? Are you tired or thinking about finishing work/practical things after they go to bed? Are you feeling rushed? If so, can you take a little bit of time for yourself before starting the bedtime rituals? Is it possible to finish the work or tasks that are on your mind *before* their bedtime routine, so you can be more relaxed and present with them? If you are wound up and in a rush, your kids can sense this and may become agitated themselves. Sometimes taking an extra half-hour or hour to finish things before we put the kids to bed can save hours of conflict afterwards. This way, you can build up more energy and go in with the right mindset.

Prepare kids for the transition

If they are playing a game or watching something before the bedtime routine begins, make sure you give them plenty of warning and the opportunity to finish what they are playing or watching. As adults, we wouldn't like it if someone just interrupted us, or turned off the TV or iPad abruptly to tell us what to do. As a general rule, try to be respectful of this. What they are doing is just as important to them as our work is to us.

> ## 🥾 Setting up their room for maximum bedtime 🥾 hygge and sleep
>
> Make going to bed something your child enjoys by ensuring their room is set up in a way that maximises the sense of hygge and promotes rest.
>
> - Arrange the area around the bed attractively so it is experienced as a positive space.
> - Let them choose the bedding and bed set-up so it feels like theirs.
> - Never send them to bed as a punishment. Bed should be a nice and cosy place they enjoy going to.
> - Air out the room before bed. Kids sleep best in a slightly cool room.
> - Dim the lighting when the bedtime ritual begins.
> - To help your child relax, try playing soft music, nature sounds or white noise.
> - If they are afraid of the dark, use a nightlight to provide a reassuring glow.

Read together

Reading doesn't only help your child become a better reader, it develops their vocabulary and ability to create sentences. A recent study conducted by Ohio State University found

that young children who were read five books a day entered
kindergarten having heard 1.4 million words more than kids
who were never read to. They concluded that this 'million-
word gap' explained the differences between vocabulary and
reading development later on. Even reading one book a day
exposes kids to more than 290,000 words more by the age of
five than those who are not read to regularly by a caregiver.

Reading all kinds of stories builds empathy

Danes are extremely honest with their children about all aspects
of life. Because of this, their children's stories touch on all kinds
of experiences – good and bad – and don't always have a happy
ending. 'The Little Mermaid' is a classic example. In the orig-
inal Danish fairy tale, the mermaid doesn't marry the prince.
She actually dies of sadness and turns into sea foam. In many
cultures, children's books only focus on happy stories in an effort
to protect them, but studies show that reading stories that feature
a range of different emotions builds empathy and resilience.

Follow and listen as you read

All children are different and observe and absorb things at
different rates. Sometimes, we can get into the habit of hush-
ing our kids if they interrupt us, because we want to read on
without being disturbed by their questions and finish the story
first. However, asking questions is how they learn and discover
that their voice and thoughts matter to us. So before reading
together, see if you can make a mental note to be open to their
curiosity and questions and follow what they see. It doesn't
matter if you finish the story; what is important is that you
acknowledge their observations and connect.

Tell them what will happen after they are put to bed

Some children at this age will be comfortable falling asleep alone, while others will need you to accompany them to sleep. If your child is comfortable falling asleep alone, tell them what will happen after they are put to bed. This way, your child is prepared for what is going to happen and like all preparation, it provides security, predictability and increases the likelihood that they will cooperate. For example, you might say:

> 'I'll come and check on you in five minutes.'
> 'I'll just be out here folding clothes while you fall asleep.'
> 'I'll come back and see you in a little while – I promise.'
> 'I'll bring you a glass of water in a little while in case you are thirsty.'

Preventing meltdowns

Bedtime is a classic moment for meltdowns – something all parents struggle with. As usual, the key is to try to stay patient and focused, and keep your big lines and the PARENT framework in mind. If you are agitated, they will be agitated. It's a cycle that comes back to us. Try to pay attention to what triggers your child so you can take preventative action as part of the bedtime routine. They might experience frustration at wanting to play longer; they may want to feel more in control; or they might have trouble communicating their needs because they have limited language. The more we understand what the triggers are (both for us and for them), the more we can prepare for these triggers and adjust the routine to avoid power struggles. When possible, pass the baton to your partner, because sometimes we all need to take a break or make a team effort to follow through on the big lines.

Bedtime with older children (7–10)

More independence

At this age, many children may like to have some time by themselves when they go to bed. Reading is a good way to get to relax and become tired. Screentime before bed is not a good idea: we know for a fact that it becomes harder to fall asleep if you watch TV, or look at an iPad or phone before bedtime. Put away screens an hour before.

Stay close

Even at this age, it is still important to be open to listening to your child before bed. Sometimes, this can mean taking your own book into their room and reading on a chair next to them, or reading to them if they still want that. Just your presence and nearness can open space for dialogue – and, of course, it is very *hyggeligt* to be together for some time at night.

Different phases

Children can go for long periods with no 'problems' going to bed, and then there comes a time where this changes. This could be due to changes in their environment: maybe they are reacting to starting school, or something is happening in the family. Sometimes their reactions to these things can even come later, when at first you'd thought there were no effects. It could also be due to developmental and psychological changes. Be aware that these phases and reactions to different stressors are normal. Get curious if something changes. Remember, there is always a meaning behind their behaviour. Some reasons for behaviour changes could be:

- **Transitions:** changes to schedules, starting school, growth spurts
- **Illness:** coughs, fevers, colds or bugs they've picked up at school
- **Family changes:** divorce, death, illness, job changes – anything that affects the family can affect development and sleep

---

👣 Precious moments 👣

Many children enjoy talking when it is time for bed. This can be true for younger kids as well as older. They may want to tell you about their experiences that day, or share some heavy thoughts about life and death. They may want to share their concerns about an ongoing conflict among the kids in school. See these as precious moments to understand your child's world, and not a ruse to stay up longer. A child's need to talk before bed often comes from the quietness of the moment. It's not always possible to talk at other times in the day, but in this calm time they can reflect and share with us. If you notice your child likes to talk before bed, try to create that nice, quiet present time earlier on. Remember that these insights into our children's minds, thoughts and concerns are gifts at any age.

Bedtime with tweens and teens (11–16)

The importance of sleep

When your child becomes a teenager, they still need a lot of sleep – two to three hours more than adults need. Going into and being in puberty is not just a big physical change. The mental development also 'goes crazy' at this time, as the brain is undergoing remodelling. From puberty to the age of twenty-two, teens need about nine hours of sleep a night. Only eight per cent of American teenagers get this amount, according to a recent study; more than half have severe sleep deprivation, sleeping on average less than six hours a night.

Getting commitment

Research shows that parental expectations really do help kids make a commitment to changing their sleep patterns. There is evidence that shows that setting limits around bedtimes, homework and media is helpful. If you haven't started your limit-setting at a younger age, it will be harder, but it's never too late to work on agreements and commitments to better sleep habits. For example, you might say:

'It's almost nine. Remember to put your phone out, like we
    agreed. The charger is in the living room.'
'Are you going to meet online with your friend after
    dinner? I know you have so much fun, it's hard to
    remember when it's time to get ready for bed. How can
    I help you? Shall I text you thirty minutes before the
    call should end, or shall I knock on the door?'

Here are some habits to encourage (not demand) to help your teen get to sleep:

- Turn off screens an hour before bed, not just to reduce the amount of blue light, which can make it harder to fall asleep, but also so they're not on social media right before bedtime.
- If possible, charge phones outside the bedroom.
- Watch the snacking, as this can postpone sleep due to sugar and caffeine.
- Don't get completely out of whack with sleep on the weekends, as this affects your entire sleep schedule – and avoid napping.
- Stop overscheduling. No one can do *everything*, and that's OK.
- Try sleep aids, such as ear plugs, eye masks or white noise.
- Keep their room at a good temperature – sleep experts say around 19°C is ideal.
- A good morning routine (see pages 110–111) will help them settle down at bedtime, as they know things will run smoothly when they wake up.

Talk about sleep

Good sleep hygiene has tremendous benefits. Teens aren't likely to change their rhythms unless they genuinely believe that more sleep will help them. A lot is happening for them right now – thoughts, feelings, friends, romantic interests, schoolwork and sports – and they need to understand that good-quality sleep can help them in all these areas. As parents, we need to involve them in the discussion and research around sleep, just like we might discuss it with our friends or other adults. We can show them that it's important to talk about sleep, and support them in putting in the effort to improve their sleep. Don't focus on the consequences of a lack of sleep, but rather the scientifically proven benefits of getting more sleep (reframing).

The benefits of good-quality sleep include:

- improved academic and sporting performance
- better cognitive function
- better concentration in everything you do
- improved ability to self-regulate aggression, impulsiveness and short-temperedness
- reduced substance abuse and risk behaviours
- improved immune function and health
- improved happiness, and reduced risk of depression

PART 3

FUN

Making time to have fun together is more important than many parents realise. It's a fundamental part of building up a child's self-esteem. Most of us believe that self-esteem and self-confidence are the same thing, but in Denmark, they make a weighty distinction between the two.

Danish teachers often explain the difference between self-confidence and self-esteem with a diagram of a tree. Self-confidence is described as the foliage of the tree. It's the things we can do or are good at. It's our accomplishments, diplomas, grades, certificates, or how popular we are. It's what everyone sees, and it's external. Self-esteem, on the other hand, is described as the roots of the tree. It's how we feel about who we are as a person, regardless of what we excel at. It's the quality of our meaningful relationships, the activities we like to do that don't require validation. It's the core of how we feel about who we are – and it's invisible to others. When we understand the real difference between self-confidence and self-esteem, it can bring on a profound paradigm shift in how we see ourselves as people and as parents.

In many cultures, it is believed that encouraging and praising children when they improve their skills and accomplish things is good for their self-esteem. The danger with this approach is that the child learns to equate love with performing, excelling or achieving, and will do whatever is required to receive that love over the course of their life. Inside, they may be thinking, *I am not good enough for who I am. I am only worthy when I do, win, earn or act in the way they want.* So their foliage appears rich and lush, but their roots are small and brittle. They may appear confident and successful to an onlooker, but what happens when the storms of life come?

Believe it or not, the simple act of playing, being in nature together, showing interest in your child's online world and inner life, making special days matter and even baking are extremely beneficial for the roots of self-esteem. When kids think, *My parents like me for who I am, and they want to be with me*, they feel deeply valued. There is a term in Danish, *at hvile i sig selv*, which means 'to rest well within yourself'. It means being able to feel good because of who you are, not what you do. You do not need to seek validation from others by showing off. This ability develops, partly, through the child believing they are lovable in the eyes of their parents and through the feedback they receive from them.

This focus on self-esteem in Denmark doesn't mean a child won't become a high-achiever. On the contrary, it means that whether they walk on the moon or walk on a beach, they will rest well within themselves. Isn't this the key to real happiness?

Nature

Parenting pitfall:
Not respecting the inner life of a child

These days, so many children are burdened with the weight of a heavy school bag and an agenda full of obligations. Every parent has a burning desire for their child to be successful, and this can lead to them grabbing every opportunity to take their kids on frenzied visits to museums, theatres, exhibitions or the like, not realising that they might be pushing for knowledge that doesn't fit into the child's inner world and maturation process. This can be stressful for the child.

In many cultures, it's desirable for kids to talk, act, dress and eat like little adults. We think it shows how clever they are. But it only takes a little awareness to realise that this drive for early development isn't about the child's experience but the parent's. I know, because I was one of those parents. The Danish way changed my perspective dramatically, especially how important free time in nature is for a child's healthy development.

From toddlers to teens, time in nature is seen as fundamental for boosting mental, spiritual and physical wellbeing. There is a strong belief that nature is the ultimate form of education for the 'whole child'. When children discover colours through the beauty of flowers in a meadow or silence through the sporadic sounds of wind rustling through trees, it's a very different learning experience, because they absorb it physiologically. Children have an innate interest in nature, so they are motivated to learn from what they are experiencing, but they do so at their own pace. Having ample time to splash in a puddle, investigate a fallen leaf in the backyard or wonder at the logistical chaos of a colony of ants is respecting the child's inner life and developmental process. This requires understanding and patience from parents.

I remember many times, on nature walks with my son, he wanted me to stop and sit down with him. He didn't say much. He would just tug my hand and point to a log, a place in the grass, or even the pavement, and I knew this was the signal for me to slow down and sit and observe our surroundings. Whenever I took the time to do this, I could literally feel him puff up with joy. What a difference those moments made to our relationship. Rather than rushing him around, pulling him to the next activity or to-do list item, I responded to his bid for connection and respected his rhythm, allowing him to explore on his own terms. Making a habit of spending time in nature helps kids set roots to *at hvile i sig selv* – 'rest well within themselves' – for the rest of their lives.

PARENT tips

Play

Nature is the ultimate playground! Kids thrive outdoors and they need risky play. Giving kids opportunities to climb trees, roll down hills, play hide-and-seek, run fast, chase each other or swing from branches is extremely beneficial for their development. Scientists believe that risky play develops fundamental mechanisms for coping with fear, which operate on the same neural pathways that help reduce stress and anxiety later in life. Thus, Danes don't look to safeguard 'dangerous' areas or overprotect kids, because they believe that children are very good at navigating scary situations and managing risk themselves. This is what fosters real self-confidence. Just be aware of the difference between a risk and a hazard. (See pages 183–186 for more about risky play.)

When you are outside, think of ways to gamify nature. See who can find the prettiest shells, or have stone-skipping contests. This is a fun way to engage everyone in play and is core to nature hygge.

Authenticity

Nature is a philosophical reflection in and of itself. It can be a wonderful place to learn about life and death, mating, sustainability, climate change, wonder and awe. Finding a dead animal or bug, for example, is something that might cause people from many cultures to say 'Eww,' or push it away and hide it from their child, but the Danish approach is the exact opposite. The idea is to be completely honest, in an age-appropriate way, about what happens in nature and in life – in all its glorious brutality and incredible vastness. Thoughts and questions about existence arise for all children as they begin to reflect on who they are in the world. What's important is that kids know that their thoughts are relevant, and that we are open to talking about them. No questions are taboo. You won't always have the answer, and that's OK. It's not about being right. It's about having conversations based on wonder and honesty.

Reframing

There is no bad weather, only bad clothing – this is one of the most classic Danish reframes. Don't let the weather stop you getting outside on any day of the year. Put on an extra coat and some rain boots, and remember it's all about perspective. Turn a fear of bugs into fascination; instead of saying, 'Yuck,' point out how many legs a spider has or how beautiful their webs are. The more fascinated and curious we are about life, the more we instil curiosity and fascination in our kids.

Empathy

Many parents don't realise that they are pushing for knowledge that doesn't fit in with the interior order of a child's inner world and maturation process. We often want them to adultify too early, encouraging them to learn facts and do lots of homework, and overscheduling them with activities. This can be stressful and anxiety-provoking. Check whether you are tuning in to your child's need to explore and study nature at their own pace. Allow them to investigate by exploring, testing, touching, tasting and feeling. Let them do so at their own pace. This creates an inner sense of peace rather than an externalised pressure to perform.

No ultimatums

Nature has a calming effect on all ages, and getting kids into nature daily reduces power struggles because it allows them to burn off energy and get the benefits of fresh air and greenery. Go prepared to get wet, cold or dirty, so you are OK with it and don't have to say, 'No.' As kids get older, we can set the tone and direction for getting outdoors. Just say, 'This is what we are doing as a family,' then make a plan and get outside for walks, hikes or bike rides. Announce it early and stick to the idea. Make it a routine and there will be less pushback. Many teens say they wish their parents would insist on getting them out more. Most of us are very happy once we are outdoors. Plan some bigger trips that involve nature, such as camping, fishing and so on, and try to involve your child's friends. This makes conflicts much less likely – and nature much more fun.

Togetherness and hygge

Spending time in nature truly goes hand in hand with the powerful effects of hygge. The sensorial experiences of being outside creates a powerful charge of excitement and makes nature very meaningful for kids. Imagine looking at it all through their eyes. Open yourself to your senses. Feel the warmth of a crackling fire on a cold night; smell the pine of a forest or hear the wind rustling through the trees. Listen to crashing waves, feel sand between your toes and smell the salty sea air of a beach. Lie in the grass and look up at the changing billowy cloud formations or feel the rough bark of a tree. What do you feel? What do you see? What do you hear? Being in nature together with your child may be one of the most profound opportunities for hygge in its truest sense. Just try it and see. It's not mindfulness – it's we-fulness.

Nature with toddlers (0–3)

Take a nature walk

One of the simplest ways to get outdoors with a toddler is to regularly go on a walk through nature. Keeping these walks predictable by visiting the same few places can have a calming quality for many kids. You could go to the park, a lake, the woods or anywhere that has some greenery. Remember a small neighbourhood park feels four times bigger to a child than it does to an adult. Natural wonders are everywhere, even in the cracks of a pavement! If you're near a pond or stream, look out for tadpoles, fish and ducks. Keep an eye out for different flowers and leaves, collect pine cones, stones or shells, or crouch down to observe the busy life of bugs.

The power of nature's hygge

Don't underestimate how awe-inspiring being in nature is for a child. Using all the senses creates a powerful charge of excitement and makes the experience very meaningful. This is nature's hygge in a nutshell.

The importance of bare feet

Danish children are encouraged to go barefoot (weather permitting) to allow to explore the sensations of being outside. There are over 200,000 nerve endings in the sole of the foot. Overwhelming studies show that small children get a host of benefits from going barefoot, from strengthening their feet to making them less prone to injury. It also helps them to more closely connect with nature. Join your child in slipping off your shoes and discover how it feels to:

- walk on grass
- wriggle your toes in sand
- walk on pebbles
- paddle in a creek
- splash in puddles

Sand, soil, water or mud

In Denmark, kids play in dirt, sand and mud all year round, regardless of the weather. There are sandpits literally everywhere. Kids who play in dirt are less likely to get sick because it strengthens their immunity, and some studies suggest that mud has antidepressant qualities that release serotonin. Only the child knows how much messiness they can tolerate, so if they seem content, embrace the mess. Children are washable, after all.

While playing in a mud kitchen, for example, your child is learning through their senses and testing out different ideas. Watch them and imagine what they are experiencing and learning as they interact with the mud.

Touch: 'What if I squish my fingers through the mud?'
Sight: 'Is my cup full? What happens if I stir it?'
Smell: 'What does it smell like?'
Sound: 'Why does it make that funny sound? Can I make it do it again?'

Pay attention to paying attention

As parents, we can all be guilty of unconsciously ignoring bids from our children to show us something (maybe because we're looking at our phones or thinking about something else). However, these bids for connection are critical to relationships. Look at the difference between these two scenarios.

Child: 'Ants! Look!'

(The child stops in wonderment and bends down to look.)

Parent: 'Be careful, the ground is dirty.'

(The parent isn't really paying attention and just spouts some conventional wisdom – the parental answering machine we talked about on page 36.)

Child: 'But look!'

(The child points excitedly, eager to show the parent.)

Parent: 'Yeah. Come on. We need to get home.'

In this example, the child feels neither seen nor heard, and a small opportunity to connect, learn and even build self-esteem is lost.

Child: 'Ants! Look!'

(The child stops in wonderment and bends down to look.)

Parent: 'Oh you're right. Look how many there are!'

(The parent stops and bends down alongside the child to see more closely.)

Parent: Oh, they are carrying a piece of food – do you see?'

In this example, the parent has followed the child's initiative and curiosity and expanded on it. The child feels seen, heard and even proud. Remember this next time you go on a walk, and try to make an effort to be present.

Make a nature table

Take a basket or jar on your nature walks so you can collect wonders to bring home and observe, such as leaves, flowers, moss, fossils or interesting stones. If it's possible to get a microscope, children can spend a lot of time studying the treasures they find (older kids will enjoy this too).

Planting seeds

Whether you do this inside or outside, planting seeds and watching the germination process is fascinating. Wrap a bean or seed in a wet paper towel or cotton wool, then check back every few days to see if it sprouts. Alternatively, plant seeds outside or in a plant pot and revisit them regularly to see if they grow.

Remember: toddlers' attention spans are shorter

Toddlers have short attention spans, and this is totally normal. Don't try to force them to learn facts or terminology just because you think they should. This is *not* hygge. Showing them something while you have their concentration is fine, as is expanding naturally on their own curiosities, but when their interest goes, let it go. Focus on experiencing and sharing their wonder, not lesson-planning.

Nature with young children (4–6)

The wonder of bugs

Discovering bugs together can be so much fun. It can feel like being nature detectives, as you explore and look for clues as a team.

- **Go on a bug hunt:** Ask your child, 'What kind of bugs do you think we can find?' Put down some white tarp and let some bugs crawl on to it or on to your hands or a stick so you can examine them more closely and foster curiosity. Talk about what you observe – 'See, the caterpillar is soft.'
- **Lift a log or large rock to see what's underneath:** Discovering creepy crawlies in nature is cool for kids. Instead of saying 'Eww' and 'Yuck,' reframe your fear as fascination. Say: 'Under this big log, there are a lot of bugs. It's humid and dark and they love it. Let's see what we can find.'
- **Make a trap:** Dig a hole and put a jar in the ground, then cover it with grass so bugs fall into the jar when they come out at night. Empty out the jar the next day in a plastic tray to see what you've caught, and talk about the different bugs: 'Wow, woodlice have so many

legs. This has (count) ... fourteen legs. How many do we have?'

Life, death and the mysteries of existence

Nature holds many joys, horrors and curiosities. Thoughts and questions about existence come up for all children as they begin to reflect on who they are and their place in the world. What's important is that they know that thoughts are relevant and that we are open to talking about them. If you come across a dead animal or bug, you might use the opportunity to talk with your child about life and death.

- **Explore the life cycle:** Dead bugs or animals can be a learning opportunity for what happens over time. Explore the food chain, decomposition, metamorphosis, and so on.
- **Allow children to express all emotions:** Be open to questions and feelings about existence without judgement. Share feelings of sympathy, fear, wonder, fascination, sadness and curiosity.
- **Read books that deal with death:** Just being able to talk about it is valuable.

👢 Risky play 👢

Enjoying risky play in nature is important for your child's development. Scientists have been studying play in animals for years, trying to understand its evolutionary purpose, and they have found that play is key for learning how to cope with stress. Resilience isn't cultivated by avoiding stress, but by learning how to tame and master it. In Denmark, children play outdoors all year round, climbing tall trees, playing near fjords, whittling with knives, making fires and sliding down muddy hills. To foreign onlookers, this can look a bit disconcerting, but risky play is seen as an absolutely essential ingredient for a healthy childhood.

Six categories of risky play that all children can benefit from

Children should not be pressured into doing these activities, but, if they want to and the activity and level of supervision is appropriate for their age, let them find and explore their own level of fear at the edge of their abilities. It's good for them!

- **Reaching new heights:** Climbing trees and other structures. The more kids push themselves, the better their brains become at regulating stress as they grow.
- **Rapid speeds:** Swinging on vines, ropes and swings; sliding down hills on sleds; running at high speeds; riding bikes fast enough to get the feeling of partly losing control. All of these improve a child's ability to cope with fear.
- **Using tools:** Using whittling knives, axes or other tools that could be potentially dangerous. This requires a tutorial so they understand how to use them.

NATURE   185

- **Exploring nature's elements:** Building a bonfire or being on the water is fascinating for kids.
- **Rough and tumble:** Chasing each other around and play-fighting in ways that seem rough to an adult. Fight-or-flight behaviours work on the same neurochemical pathways in the brain that stress does, making them more resilient.
- **Disappearing/getting lost:** Playing hide-and-seek and experiencing the thrill of separation from friends and family, or, for older kids, exploring on their own. Danes believe that all children like to hide away from adults in play, which must be respected. It is innate (not sneaky).

Be aware! A risk is not the same as a hazard

A child deciding to climb up a tree is a risk. It's manageable, and they have to actively make a decision about how much risk they want to take (i.e. how high they will climb). This is how they learn to manage stress. Climbing up a tall tree that has a rotten branch, on the other hand, is a hazard, because there is a real threat and it is dangerous. Be aware of genuine hazards versus risks.

Skinned knees are a part of life

Children are far more competent than many give them credit for. In Denmark, parents don't try to safeguard everything, but explain to their children what they need to be careful of and trust that their kids can figure it out (within reason). Many playgrounds in the US, on the contrary, have become so protective and 'safe' that the children misuse the equipment to try and make it more risky (and therefore more fun)!

Reframing fear as a parent

Focus on your child's experience of fun, rather than your experience of worry. The next time you are in nature with your child and instinctively want to yell out, 'Be careful,' 'No,' or 'Stop,' try to take a breath and ask yourself, 'How can I convey more trust and support rather than fear and worry?'

You could encourage them to check in with their feelings and senses and think about ways to play safely by saying things like:

'Notice how . . . those rocks are slippery/the log is rotten/ that branch is strong.'

'Try moving . . . more slowly/carefully/quickly/strongly.'

'Try using your . . . hands/feet/arms/legs.'

'Can you hear . . . the rushing water/the singing birds/the wind?'

'Do you feel . . . stable on that rock/the heat from the fire?'

'Are you feeling . . . scared/excited/tired/safe?'

'What's your plan if you . . . climb that boulder/cross that log?'

'What can you use . . . to get across/for your adventure?'

'Where will you . . . put that rock/move to next?'

'How will you . . . get down/go up/get across?'

Nature with older children (7–10)

The benefits of nature

Research clearly shows that kids who spend time out in nature are:

- calmer
- healthier
- better students
- less likely to be overweight

They're also likely to have better vision.

Join the Scouts

Joining the Scouts or similar groups is a fantastic way to get kids in contact with nature, and also allows them to learn survival skills, engage in risky play (see box above) and practise teamwork. If there are Scout groups in your area, I highly recommend getting involved.

Making nature fun

Danes are truly excellent at coming up with playful competitions to enjoy in nature, making family hygge time more fun as everyone becomes more engaged. Keep an eye out for opportunities to invent games – here are some ideas to get you started.

Skipping stones	Everyone chooses three stones for skipping, then competes to see who can skip them the furthest (with most skips). It's fun to discuss the stones' shapes and sizes, and hypothesise on which ones will work best.
Nature bingo	Make a nature bingo board based on finding different things: leaves, insects, flowers, etc. (This is a really popular activity in Danish schools.)
Find the prettiest stone or shell	Split up into teams and search for the prettiest or most interesting shells or stones. Put them in a pile anonymously and then vote for the top three without knowing who picked what. There are many variations on this.
Crab racing	Catch crabs and then dig lanes in the sand to the sea and bet on whose crab will make it back to the sea fastest.
Scavenger hunts	Everyone gets a jar and has to try and find five different things to share. For example, you could say that everyone has to find a funny-shaped leaf, something red, something soft, something round and something pretty.

Making nature or land art

Take a piece of paper outside and sit and draw or paint with materials from nature. Squish leaves, flowers and berries, and use them as crayons and paints. This is a lovely way to explore and experience art with the senses. Talk to your child about the shapes, textures, forms and colours you find. Here are some examples of nature's palette:

- **green:** leaves, grass and peas
- **yellow:** flowers, fruits or lemons
- **red, blue and purple:** berries or fruits
- **brown:** bark and mud
- **grey:** stones and moss

Read books about nature

Kids are fascinated by dangerous animals and interesting facts or records they can read over and over again (my kids absolutely loved these). Find out what is interesting to your child. The key is not to overwhelm them with text. Popular themes for Danish children are:

• the world's most dangerous animals
• the world's weirdest animals
• the world's funniest animals
• World records in nature

Build a little aquarium

Bringing tadpoles in from the outside and putting them in an aquarium can be fascinating to watch. It's a wonderful story of metamorphosis. You can also collect different kinds of bugs or leaves or sticks to put in the aquarium.

Camping

Going camping is an incredible bonding activity for families. Camping teaches so many teamwork skills as you work together to set up the tents, build the fire (see below), prepare food and clean up. This builds confidence and self-esteem. Camping also presents numerous opportunities for nature walks, hikes, fishing and scavenger hunts, as well as giving you the chance to really turn off and tune in to hygge together. There is also ample opportunity for risky play (see box pages 183–186)!

BUILDING A CAMPFIRE

Building a fire together is a magical experience. It provides warmth on a cold evening, and it allows us to cook food outside. For thousands of years, humans have told stories by the light of a fire, so after you've eaten, gather around the flames to tell stories, sing songs or simply pause to enjoy the silence.

Learning to build a fire gives a child an incredible sense of confidence, which is one of the reasons it's an integral part of Danish education. Most Danish children are already building fires in kindergarten, and will build many more throughout their lives. Children are taught that they must have respect for fire because it is dangerous.

Here are some tips so you can enjoy your campfire safely:

- Make your fire in designated fireplaces or somewhere you know is safe.
- Don't light a fire if the forest floor is very dry, as it risks getting out of control.
- Never light a fire without an adult present.
- Don't run around the fire or throw things into it. Sit at a good distance.
- Always have water by the fire and remember to put it out thoroughly. Even small unextinguished embers can spark up again during the night.

TORCHLIGHT WALKS

Going camping gives you the chance to experience nature in the dark. Make the most of it by heading out at night or early in the morning with a torch. Once you've been walking for a while, stop and turn off the torch, then spend a moment getting used to the dark. See the silhouettes of the trees and surroundings, listen to and observe the sounds around you, and soak up the atmosphere together. It can be a little scary but also exciting.

EXPLORE THE PATH NOT TAKEN

Use your camping trip to take a tour off the beaten path. Walk through a creek, climb up a hill, run away together and climb over some fallen trees, or balance on a log. Your child may get scratches, bruises and wet feet, but these are the bodily experiences of being in nature.

Nature with tweens and teens (11–16)

Nature therapy

Many children in this age group say they sometimes feel trapped in themselves, caught up in their thoughts and feelings. They question how they feel and worry that they don't have solutions. Being in nature has a very positive effect on these thoughts and feelings, because teens are able to come out of themselves in the vastness. Studies show that walks in nature reduce our tendency to ruminate. Nature therapy is prescribed around the world to battle anxiety and a host of other problems.

Just do it!

Rather than wait for the desire to come from your kids, just plan it and say, 'Now, this is what we are doing as a family. We are going out for a walk.' It's almost always going to be a good idea to get some fresh air and be outside in some way, shape or form. It also creates opportunities to have conversations you wouldn't be able to have otherwise. Nature as a family – just do it. Here are some ideas:

- walks in the forest, at the beach or in a park
- bike rides
- picnics (bring outdoor games like frisbee or ball games)
- short hikes

Engage their interests

Involve your teens in the decision-making around nature adventures and encourage them to invite their friends. This makes it more fun to go on long hikes or try 'tougher' excursions together. Plan special outings so it becomes a tradition a few times a year. Use or designate a nature guide when needed. You could try:

- hiking
- canoeing or kayaking
- white-water rafting
- camping
- fishing
- snorkelling or diving
- bushcraft

Nature and technology

The two are not mutually exclusive and mixing them can help tweens and teens to become more interested in and engaged with nature. Do some research based around what they like. Here are some ideas.

Nature apps	There are apps that can identify bird calls, plants, flowers, insects and wildlife, and that offer ways to record and save observations.
Geocaching	Find treasures all over the world with a GPS system.
Stargazing apps	Apps like *Star Walk 2* show you what stars are above you, around you and even 'beneath' you on the other side of the Earth. Wonderful for camping.
Get magnifying	There are apps that turn technology into magnifying glasses and microscopes, enabling children to look into the world of nature.
Pokémon GO	An old classic, but a fun way to go exploring deep into nature by catching Pokémon. Just keep a balance between enjoying the game and being in and paying attention to your surroundings.

Summer camps

Summer camps can be transformative experiences for kids. There are many different kinds, so look into what is best for your child. Your teens can benefit from:

- improved independence
- gaining the courage to overcome fears and try new things
- working together with their peers
- making new friends
- being in nature

Familiehøjskole (family camps)

These are camps for the whole family that you can go to in

the summer. There are activities for the adults (fitness, sailing, yoga, Nordic walking and so on) and for the kids (nature excursions, biking, dance, survival games, swimming), and then some activities for the whole family. A lot of the camps are nature-based and activities are divided by age, so whether you have a younger child or a teen, their interest will be captured. These camps are a really nice way to be together, and are becoming more popular in other countries.

Screentime

Parenting pitfall:
Feeling scared? Don't say 'no', say 'know'

I was absolutely terrified when my daughter wanted to get her first smartphone and have more freedom in the online world. There were so many mental health issues associated with social media, along with my anxieties around screentime addiction, the impact it might have on her sleep, and her potentially having access to inappropriate content. I felt overwhelmed and underprepared. We were not living in Denmark at the time, and she wasn't learning from the *digital dannelse* (the Danish digital citizenship programme in school), which I knew was very good. The goal of this programme is to teach kids how to be kind, careful, competent, safe and decent online citizens – just like we aim to teach them to be in the real world. The process is very much based on building trust, rather than inciting fear. Denmark is voted as having some of the highest levels of digital wellbeing in the world, and this is partly due to the fact that they have embraced technology rather than demonising it. I knew my daughter and I needed to have many conversations to prepare her (and myself), but how and where would I start?

I decided to create a set of conversation cards, based on the

Danish programme. These cards are a playful way to cover topics like consent, critical thinking, bullying, gaming, social media use and much more. We agreed that she could get a phone and gain access to more online freedoms once we had gone through the cards and made an agreement together. They took us a few weeks to complete, but we had so many interesting discussions. I learned as much as she did, and I felt certain that she knew how to handle many difficult situations and could think more critically for herself. Most importantly, we were aligned on our family's values.

Many parents take for granted that their children will know how to navigate and stay safe in the digital world, but unless we talk about it at home, they don't. To this day, I am extremely happy with how we approached this important rite of passage. It required an investment of time as a parent, but if I had catastrophised it or overcontrolled it, we wouldn't have built the trusting relationship we have today – which I am convinced is much more protective than restriction would have been. Reframing 'no' into 'know' can also make a tremendous difference in the teen years.

PARENT tips

Play

Playing on screens can be like a digital sandpit for kids. Just as we wouldn't leave our little ones all alone on a playground, don't leave them alone online. As they get older, show interest in and learn about what they are playing. Games that are social and bridge the physical and digital worlds are usually creative. Step outside your comfort zone and look for something you can play together. Learn the terminology of their games and ask to play. What does the slang they use mean? Make sure they know some basic safety rules around apps, purchases, strangers and dealing with conflict in games. Think less about controlling screentime and more about quality play on the screen. If our children were reading books, building robots or studying, we wouldn't be upset about them spending a lot of time doing that. So, let's help them find good games and online activities that are worth their time. Remember to praise them for healthy digital play.

Authenticity

Are you walking the walk and talking the talk? Are you exhibiting the same habits you would like to see in your children? We can't expect our kids to respect rules if we don't respect them ourselves. Children mirror us, so let's give them something good to imitate. Answer these questions honestly, and return to them regularly:

- Am I able to be present in my environment when I am not on my computer or phone?
- Do I sit in front of a computer for many hours in a row without a break?
- Do I send messages, answer the phone, read updates on social media, look at emails, etc, when the family is together?
- Do I film small or big moments and share them on social media without thinking about it?
- Do I share with my child what I am doing on my phone, telling them what I am looking up on the net or what game I am playing?
- Do I have a public profile on, for example, Facebook or Instagram?

- Do I share pictures of my kids (and other people's kids) on social media without asking them first?
- Are there any media-free zones or times in the house (such as mealtimes), and do I respect them myself?

Reframe

As I shared above, don't say 'no', say 'know'. As humans, we tend to focus on the negative aspects of a situation. This is called negativity bias, and it is part of our evolutionarily programming because, historically, it helped us survive. It meant we could spot snakes and life-threatening things. This is one of the reasons why parents tend to instinctively react with fear and suspicion when considering their children's tech use, and often want to quash it or control it. The digital landscape is very scary for us, and while this is completely understandable from a psychological perspective, it doesn't help to engage with this fear, because this is the world in which our kids are living. They need to learn to navigate the digital landscape and fend for themselves. When we reframe and focus on the positive opportunities rather than the threats, our kids are much more willing to talk with us, which is really the best protection. So the next time you instinctively feel yourself thinking the worst and saying 'no', get curious and say 'know'. Try to learn more about it. The more we show interest in their online world rather than reacting with fear, the easier it is to keep an open line of communication.

Empathy

In the same way we teach children how to read others and behave empathetically in the real world, Danes do this in the digital world as well. They call it *den gode tone* or 'the good tone'. Remember that it can be very difficult to 'read' people's emotions when you can't see them in person to interpret their tone of voice and body language. Talking about good online communication is crucial to help avoid misunderstandings and develop digital empathy. Ask your child about their online friends and experiences, just as you would ask them about friends and experiences in school or after school. Help them solve conflicts and learn basic rules of communication with kindness. Try to acknowledge what your child tells you with openness and sincerity, not judgement or moralising. For example: 'Oh, that's interesting,' or 'Hmmm, I didn't think of that. What do you mean?' By listening more and recognising our children's ideas first, and only then helping them consider more options, they learn to trust their instincts rather than just telling you what they think you want to hear.

No ultimatums

It can be tempting to threaten with ultimatums to take away phones or technology but remember the big lines of parenting and what you want to achieve. Is blocking their social life and sense of belonging the most respectful and effective way of upholding boundaries in the long run? Is demanding their password and reading their messages building the trust so necessary in the digital world as they get older? For younger kids, make sure to have parental locks on and be very clear on screentime limits. As they get older, make agreements about rules, boundaries and consequences. Use the agreement they have been a part of making to avoid power struggles and maintain equal dignity. Threats, fear and blame are not conducive to respect. Only respect is conducive to respect. It's a cycle that comes back to you. Remember that if you choose to constantly see your child as sneaky, manipulative and untrustworthy, it may become a self-fulfilling prophecy.

Togetherness and hygge

Set up the living room so it's a cosy space where kids and parents feel welcome to be on their screens in the same room for a designated amount of time, either sitting on sofas or at the table. Consider it 'digital hygge'. It's a bit like if you were all reading a book in the same room. This way, you can still chat and share what you are doing or reading about online, while enjoying a cup of tea or something nice to eat. It is the idea of being 'alone together' and it's still cosy. There should also be designated screen-free times for meals, play, homework, etc, but being on screens doesn't mean we have to hide away in our rooms or offices.

Screentime for toddlers (0–3)

Limit screentime for toddlers as much as possible

It is recommended by the Danish Ministry of Health* that kids under two years old don't use screens except to communicate with relatives. Danish recommendations don't forbid screens, but rather suggest using them in an intelligent way, especially for the youngest children. Some ideas could be:

---

* As with many countries, guidelines are frequently changing. The information provided reflects the most recent recommendations at the time of writing.

- watching something appropriate for toddlers
- listening to music
- watching and listening to something with simple sounds and visuals – nothing too high tempo or noisy
- finger-drawing on screen

Always bring other toys

At this age, play is considered the most important activity a child can engage in, and the screen can easily become a babysitter when you're out to eat, running errands or visiting with friends. Toddlers will happily play with other things if they have an option. Make sure to pack some toys or art material wherever you go, so you don't default to a screen.

Free play is best

Make sure children get as much movement and time away from screens as possible, both indoors and outdoors in nature, where their wonder, awe and imagination can flourish. Building free play into daily routines helps you to avoid a reliance on screens.

Screentime for younger children (4–6)

Set screen limits that *you* can respect

Ideally kids of this age will be on screens as little as possible. However, if they do use screens, prioritise being with them as much as possible, and try to only set screentime limits if you *know* you will be able to respect them. Otherwise, you will teach them that 'no' doesn't actually *mean* 'no', which can become a nightmare. Here are some tips.

🥾 Some good standard guidelines for 🥾 younger children around screentime

- Make sure children get adequate time for play, movement and socialising offline. This is critical for their development.
- Avoid high-tempo games and apps with very distracting content.
- Keep meals, bedtimes and plenty of playtime free from screens.
- Do not use screens an hour before bedtime, as this risks disturbing sleep.
- Make sure devices have the latest parental locks and privacy controls.

The digital world feels very real for our kids

The virtual space is just another play space for our kids. They have grown up with it and, in their minds, being online is as normal as running around the house playing tag or reading a book. When children move seamlessly between the two worlds, it's called fluid play. Researchers have seen many of the same benefits of play in the digital world as they see in the real world. The more we understand this, the easier it is to see opportunities rather than obstacles in this new form of play.

Play on screens together

Most parents recognise the importance of playing with their children, but the majority of us haven't included digital play in that equation. We are generally happy to play board games or toss a ball around, but we often leave kids alone to play with the phone, tablet or computer. While this is perfectly fine sometimes, they also need 'family play' in the digital world. Watching movies together or playing online games is recommended in Denmark.

Research appropriate and fun games and apps

Games and apps are developing all the time, so make an effort to learn about what you want to put on a screen for your child to use. Every child is unique, so depending on what they might be interested in, look for things that are not mindless games or shows designed to hold attention at all costs. There is a lot of good stuff out there, but we need to do our research and avoid games and apps that feature a lot of ads that target children as consumers. Make sure they don't have access to anything outside what you choose at this age.

Media-free zones

These are places and times when everyone – including children, parents, other family members, friends and caregivers – turns off their screens, and it's important we *all* respect this. This can be at mealtimes and during 'play' time or designated quiet time, and for one hour before bed. These times and/or zones can be decided together as a family but it's important to follow through.

Bring other toys when you go out

I can't reiterate this enough. Just as you do for toddlers, do this for your younger children. Remember to pack other toys and encourage real-life interactions whenever possible.

Screentime for older children (7–10)

'You will never know as much as your kids'

This is the message in Denmark. It's better that we, as parents, accept this and learn from them as we guide them with the big message of how to be good digital citizens rather than trying to control them.

🥾 Think quality versus quantity 🥾

Parents often focus on controlling screentime, but technology has many positive aspects and possibilities. When we acknowledge our child's fascination with the digital world, we can help them find high-quality uses of technology instead of mindless ones. Some examples could be:

- being creative – such as making movies, art or music
- learning something new, like coding, chess or design
- talking to friends and collaborating on homework
- playing educational games

Talk to your child about their online life

Remember that the digital world is a real place for children, and they have to deal with real challenges there. Talk to them about their online life, just as you would their day at school.

FIND OPPORTUNITIES TO TALK ABOUT WHAT THEY PLAY ONLINE

So many parents have no idea what our kids are playing online. There is a tendency to stay away from things we don't know, but it is so important to get involved. Don't be afraid – be curious about it. This is how we stay close to our children. Normalise sitting next to them while they're online, even if you are doing something else. You'll be amazed how much they appreciate it. If they are gaming, for example, ask about the characters and purpose.

'Why do you like that character or avatar?'
'What can they do?'
'What are their special powers?'

LEARN THE TERMINOLOGY

Learn their digital terminology. Kids generally think it's really funny when parents are able to use their language in conversation, and it makes you feel more connected. Bridge the gap between their online worlds and the real world by asking them things like:

'What's a "skin"?'
'What are "virtual objects"?'

'What do the different acronyms used in this game mean?'
'What does the slang mean that you're using in your
    online communication?'

Play games together

Ask if you can follow along in their games, or see if there is a
game you can join in with. Suggest a game you might both like.
Have fun! Whatever kind of digital play they are interested in,
try to learn about it and be a part of it, just as you would in the
'real' world. Kids love when their parents get silly and involved.

Avoid time on screens becoming too solitary

Many of the afternoon play schools and clubs in Denmark do
have screens and technology, but they generally don't condone
gaming alone. They often have a big screen or TV so kids can
all play together.*

A Danish rule of thumb for screentime is that online games
should offer a good mix of creative, physical, social and digital play. Games that encourage physical movement, like Wii
games or *Just Dance*, are good examples of this mix.

Encourage reflection in digital play and gaming

If your child is into gaming, make sure to discuss how to
resolve conflicts if they come up in digital play with friends.
Some good discussion points are:

---

* As with many countries, guidelines are frequently changing. The information provided reflects the most recent recommendations at the time of
writing.

- When is language too harsh?
- How should you deal with strangers, and who is it OK to befriend in games?
- When should you block or mute someone?
- What are pranks, and when are they OK – and not OK? (This is important because pranks can be fun and funny, but they can also wreak havoc. Kids often don't know the difference.)

Teach honesty

Make honesty a value and talk about how important it is. Your child should know that they can *always* come to you (or another trusted adult) if something difficult happens, even if it's something they think is wrong or are worried you might be angry about. We all make mistakes. This is how we learn.

👢 Safety basics 👢

Give your child guidance on online safety, just as you prepare them to be safe in the physical world. Some basics to cover include:

- Remember that you never know who's who in the online world.
- Don't share your personal information – for example, full name, address, phone number, parent's info – with anyone.
- Beware if someone you meet online offers you gifts for no reason.
- Never meet up with someone you don't know in real life.

> • Know which adults to go to if something unpleasant
> happens – parents, a teacher, etc.

Teach critical thinking

We so often take critical-thinking skills for granted, but it's important to talk about things like how to interpret hidden ads or touched-up photos, how to identify misleading promises or fake profiles, and how to spot scams, AI, fake news and more. Ensure your child knows:

- that many images are filtered, photoshopped or fake
- that influencers are paid to advertise
- the benefits and risks of AI
- the difference between hidden ads and obvious ones
- how to spot fake news
- how to identify phishing scams (false messages and emails promising you money or prizes that can compromise your accounts)
- about hidden costs in apps and games (discuss online purchases as part of your screentime agreements)

LOOK FOR EXAMPLES OF CRITICAL-THINKING OPPORTUNITIES IN EVERYDAY LIFE

Try to keep the conversation going. We want our kids to be confident, capable and good critical thinkers, even when we aren't there to protect them. Practice makes perfect, so keep talking about it.

Be curious, not furious

If you see your child looking at something you think they shouldn't, remain calm and ask questions like, 'How did you get to that webpage?' or 'What did you click on?' We want to help them become good digital citizens, not punish them for curiosity. It may be that your child has clicked on something by mistake – or they may have gone looking for this very content having heard about it from friends. Children are naturally curious and may search for things without understanding what they might find.

Screentime for tweens and teenagers (11–16)

Conversations are the best protection

Research firmly supports the idea that open and honest con-versations are the best long-term protection in the digital world, and are far more effective than fear and control. These discussions are not about 'telling' kids what's right or wrong or scaring them, but instead beginning a dialogue between you that will last for life.

Tweens and teens have a right to a private life

In Denmark, it is firmly believed that at this age, it's a child's right to have a private life: to close their door and have things their parents don't know about. This can be difficult for many parents, especially when we are scared, but it's really about respecting who our child is becoming. Some parents only allow kids to use certain social media sites as long as they can always check their accounts and messages at any time. Think about how you would feel if someone did this to you. Yes, there should be agreements on what is OK and not OK for their age, but the idea is to create trust. Here are some good rules of thumb:

- Have open conversations and make agreements about what they can or can't do online.
- Don't try to control everything on their phone.
- Don't access and read their messages or check their accounts.
- Don't demand their passwords. In Denmark, this is considered a violation of privacy. It is not basing the relationship on trust.
- If you are concerned, openly ask about what is going on.

Some Danes do use tracking apps. This is generally in agreement with the child, and with the understanding that parents won't use them all the time. No one wants to feel they are being monitored at every moment.

Don't catastrophise

Catastrophising doesn't encourage kids to open up to us, because they are afraid of losing their access to a social life. Saying things like, 'See, I told you it's dangerous and evil,' and 'We should ban all phones and social media,' just makes kids feel alone in the digital landscape, and may leave them reluctant to come to us if something bad happens – which is far more dangerous.

Teach them about their digital footprint

Every time your child visits a site on the internet or clicks through to see other sites or share information, pictures or commentary, it is collected as data and a digital footprint is made. We can never be 100 per cent sure that anything we post, comment or look at goes away, so your child should be very critical of what they post and look for. This can affect future job and study opportunities.

Talk about consent

Discuss what consent means and why it's so important, particularly when it comes to taking and sending photos and videos. Make sure your teen understands that they shouldn't take and share photos of other people if they haven't consented, and talk about the potential consequences of sharing private material without consent (which can range from nothing at all to extremely serious, depending on what that material is).

Be a good role model: ask your child for consent before posting or sharing any images or videos of them, so that they see this as standard behaviour. Kids mirror their parents, so your example matters, and this will be reflected in their interactions, drama and friendships.

Be sincere, not judgemental

When you have conversations with your child about things you find difficult (rules, privacy, porn, sexting, etc), prepare yourself in advance so that you can be open and sincere and not patronising, moralistic or judgemental. Our language and tone make a huge difference.

🦵 **What does wellbeing and screen use look like?** 🦵

Discuss the effects of screentime on the brain and body.
Teens can easily have these kinds of discussions. Talk about
what media boundaries look like and why it's important
to respect them. First and foremost, make sure you are
modelling the behaviour you want to see. Ask yourself the
following questions so you are able to discuss them honestly
and openly with your teen:

- What are my media boundaries? What about those of
  my friends?
- How can I keep track of my phone use?
- How do I feel after scrolling for hours?
- How can I improve my wellbeing?
- Why is it dangerous to focus on followers and likes?

Screen overuse

Discuss how to keep an eye out for signs of problematic screen
use and have some strategies for what to do.

Signs of overuse include:

- feeling nervous when they have no access to screens,
  games or social media
- screens or social media taking priority over 'real' life
- feeling obsessed with likes and followers
- needing to constantly check their phone
- preferring to spend time on social media rather than
  have connection in the real world

If your child is struggling with social media or screen addiction, here are some things they could try:

- Acknowledge the signs (such as anxiety, red eyes, irritability or sleep disturbance). Awareness is the first step.
- Take a break and do something else. Remember, likes and followers are not a reflection of reality.
- Put down the phone and go outside. Revisit media boundaries to schedule more breaks.
- Meet up with friends or family in person. Human connection is extremely important.
- Talk to a trusted adult if it feels serious.

The importance of digital empathy

Den gode tone, or the good tone, is a big focus in Denmark. Here are some rules of thumb:

- **Don't ever send mean messages:** This can make people sad and upset.
- **Don't like or comment on mean messages:** This can feel like you have sent or written the message yourself.
- **Invite everyone around you to see what you're looking at on your phone or computer:** This way, people don't feel excluded (this is an important habit for family members as well).
- **Get consent:** Only share films or pictures of others if you have been given permission by them.
- **Get help:** If you or someone you know is a victim of cyber-bullying, get help from an adult.

Reacting versus responding

It's a good idea to take some time to cool down and reflect before writing comments or sending messages if you feel upset. Reacting without thinking can create so many unnecessary problems. Practise looking for meaning behind online behaviour rather than judging or assuming the worst.

Help your child (and yourself), consider this before reacting:

'Maybe they had a bad day.'	Think the best of people. It will make you feel better and help you communicate better.
'Maybe they couldn't write back immediately.'	People are busy. Just because a message looks read, doesn't mean they can respond.
'Maybe they didn't use the right emojis.'	It's very hard to read what others mean online because we can't see facial expressions or hear their tone of voice. If you aren't sure what someone meant, call and ask.
When in doubt, ask first, don't react	Rather than reacting negatively, call the person or speak to them to ask what they meant.

Be vulnerable and share

If your child calls you out on your own digital behaviour – for things like not respecting media boundaries or consent rules, for example – then own up to it. At this age, they are hypocrisy detectors. Share times when you may have felt addicted to the phone, been distracted by your screen or misunderstood someone else's message. When you apologise and admit you don't have all the answers, you show your kids that you are human. Be vulnerable and admit when you make mistakes.

This lets them know that they can come to you and be honest when they do the same.

> ♊ **Raising digital citizens conversation cards** ♊
>
> We can't recommend these highly enough. Kids love it when their parents show genuine interest in their digital lives (rather than just negativity). It's hygge, not homework, so the experience should be pleasant, not a task. Treat your child as a partner, not a pupil (see page 62) and let the conversations flow naturally. Countless parents around the globe have had great success improving their relationship with their children using the cards, and kids love it too. raisingdigitalcitizens.com

Make agreements *together*

Studies clearly show that children from families who govern with respect and inclusion are far more likely to be influenced by their parents, not their peers. Once you feel you have had enough conversations about digital citizenship, make an agreement together with your child – don't hand them something to sign that is already made. It's important they are involved. The agreement can be updated as they get older, and it could include:

- **Setting media boundaries:** What, when and how much screentime is OK.
- **Respecting self:** The difference between quality versus quantity when it comes to screentime, and how to measure use and get screen-free time.

- **Respecting others:** Basic rules of respect in communication ('the good tone').
- **Basic care:** Treating devices with respect.
- **What to do:** If something upsetting happens, who to go to.
- **Consequences:** What will happen if the agreement is not kept (these should come from the child)

Indoor play

Parenting pitfall: Not prioritising play

When my daughter was little, I was obsessed with getting any toy that could help her read or learn numbers faster. We watched shows that were 'educational', and I was researching schools and universities before she was in pre-school. After many strange looks from my husband, some long discussions and seeing how differently childhood was viewed in Denmark, I began to see another way. In Denmark, free play is considered the absolute most important activity a child can engage in. The majority of Danes find the idea of over-scheduling a child's life with learning and adult-led activities a bit odd. The attitude is that if children are always performing to obtain something – such as good grades, or praise from teachers, coaches and parents – how do they learn to develop their own sense of self, true creativity and inner drive? There are no pedestals in play, no special praise, no trophies. Kids are motivated by their own desire to keep the game alive and their imaginations. Free play has been proven to teach many skills: critical thinking, negotiation, empathy, grit and self-control, to name a few. But this learning comes from the child, not an adult.

These days, it can almost feel like you are depriving your child if you are not enrolling them in myriad courses: swimming, yoga, tennis, dance, piano, Spanish, organic cupcake-making and so on. I think most parents have found themselves wondering 'Am I doing enough?' when they hear what other kids are 'taking' in their spare time. A better question would be: 'Who are we doing this *for*?' Are we really doing it for our kids' internal development, or is it because we feel pressured by other parents to do it? We sometimes forget that what children want most of all is to feel calm and good with their parents. They need time to act out what they experience in the adult world, to take in life and reflect. They need time to decompress from their days and to feel loved even when they aren't performing. It wasn't until I finally believed in the power of play that I was able to relax and let go. Rather than seeing my daughter's childhood as a race to prepare for her future and control it, I saw it as incredibly sacred time to protect. It was a huge paradigm shift for me, and I could see how much happier she was. In truth, I was happier too. It's often the more 'educated' parents who feel under pressure to constantly develop their kids as a subtle sign of their own success. But what if we discovered that play was actually the most educated choice of all?

PARENT tips

Play

Play looks different for small children and teens, but the underlying structure is the same, and it's good to keep in mind. Dr

Peter Gray, one of the world's leading play experts, has defined play as follows:

- **It is voluntary or self-directed:** This means the child chooses how and what to play. This is how they learn to take charge, initiate and direct activities in life. When adults get too involved in child's play, or a teacher or coach directs it, it's not fully play.
- **It is intrinsically motivated:** Play is done for the sake of play rather than for a reward or praise. Play may have goals, but the goal is part of the process, not the result. For example, playing with building blocks or LEGO may include the goal of building something, but the main objective is in the creating, not in having the finished product.
- **It is guided by mental rules:** Play always has some rules created by the player(s) which form the boundaries. In fantasy play, for example, it is understood you are supposed to stay in character. Maybe you are the cat who meows or the teacher who runs the class. Play-fighting may look wild, but there is usually an understanding not to hurt each other.
- **It is creative and imaginative:** This is the ability to enter an imaginary world and be creative. The rules of play don't necessarily have anything to do with reality.
- **You can quit:** As most children are intrinsically motivated to play, they want to keep it going. But a defining characteristic of play is that you can quit. If you can't quit, it's not play.

Play for older children will look different than play for small kids, but it has a similar structure in that it is self-chosen, self-driven, has some rules and is creative. Give teens ample opportunity to play things they like that aren't tied up with your identity or with the sole purpose of winning. If you help them tap in to their intrinsic playful drive, it could become a hobby for life.

Play activities can be found in the appendix (pages 283–289).

Authenticity

What did you like to play with when you were little? Really think back. Dolls? Cars? Physical or rough-and-tumble play? Children love to see us being sincere, interested in and enthusiastic about play. The more you can be in touch with your inner *legebarn* (your 'inner play child') the better.

Be honest when you aren't in the mood. It's better to let your child know that you've had a long day or are too tired to play. It's totally OK to be honest. See if there is a way to be involved while resting. You could say:

'Let's lie on the sofa and you can show me how your dolls
   play.'
'Let's play "What's on my back?" I'll lie down and you put
   some toys on my back, and I have to guess what they are.'

Just try to balance those days out with days you do play in a more involved and engaged way. Be a playmate, not a prop. Include yourself and what you like to play, too. If we always play only what our child wants, with no negotiation or compromise, this won't help them when they play with other children, who most likely won't stand to be bossed around.

Reframe

Some parents really do enjoy playing, but many of us have a limited capacity for it. Thinking that you 'aren't good' at playing or that you 'should' play are thoughts that, by their very nature, rob you of playfulness. You will find that when you stop pressuring yourself, it will all go much easier.

Learning to lose is a positive and important experience. It's normal to feel frustration when we lose, but it's how we deal with that frustration that matters. Remember the reframe acronym FAIL: first attempt in learning. If we model that it's human to fail and that there are many other positive things to focus on, our children will be gentler on themselves when they fail, and not see it as a terrible thing. Board games and card games are great ways for kids to practise winning and losing. If your child gets very upset, try more collaborative games, like charades or Pictionary, where you can be on the same team. This way, you model being good winners and good losers together. Try to be a realistic optimist: acknowledge that your child lost and it sucked (reality), but also remind them of other times they've played well and how good that felt.

Empathy

Tune in to their mood. Does your child need some quiet time playing alone, or do they need to burn some energy? Tuning in to each other helps us understand what kind of play is best for the moment.

Role play is one way to develop social skills and empathy. 'Teaching' empathy should never be a goal in play, but modelling sharing, soothing and being polite naturally develops social skills.

We also know that children (all humans) thrive on physical connection. The power of touch releases oxytocin, which improves feelings of wellbeing and increases trust. Even if you come from a family that was not very affectionate, believe in the benefits of touch and try to be more aware of creating opportunities for contact through play: have a spa day, play tag, braid their hair, etc. Give your child a pat on the back, a high five, a hug – and remember, especially in group play or team sports, to compliment other children who are playing, and not just your own child.

No ultimatums

Make sure kids get enough physical play. This can help reduce conflicts. Danish schools often have kids run laps or do physical activity to reduce power struggles.

Before you enter into an argument with your child because they want to quit doing an organised activity, remember that it's normal to go through phases. Your teen may suddenly stop playing the piano or doing sports in which they have acquired great skills after many years. This very often happens from the ages of thirteen to fifteen, as teens naturally push away from what their parents want (so be prepared). Sometimes it's OK to let them have a break and try something else. Don't make the activity about the money you've spent. Make it about the agreements and commitments you have made together in advance, and be open to listening and making new agreements.

Togetherness and hygge

Hygge is how we improve feelings of belonging. A major goal for Danish parents in play is that kids learn how to feel good together as a group: 'we win' versus 'I win'. Praising kids for how well they work together, take care of each other and listen to each other will foster togetherness rather than individualism. Research shows that we are happier when we win together rather than winning alone.

A lot of time is devoted to groups having hygge together outside of training, games or performances. Cosying around having pizza, playing board games or taking trips together is fundamental, because it creates a sense of *fællesskab* ('community'). This is true for the parents as well. When you genuinely feel that you like each other off the field, you play and perform better on it.

Indoor play with toddlers (0–3)

Toy minimalism

The Danish government recommends having fewer toys, as studies show that toddlers play longer, and are more concentrated and creative, when they have fewer toys. Four, for example, is better than sixteen. Rotate them out and bring them back in, and they will seem like new to your child.

Opportunities for play are everywhere

See the world through your toddler's eyes, and you will see opportunities everywhere that go far beyond store-bought toys. My two-year-old niece recently spent a solid twenty minutes deeply concentrated on taking headphones in and out of their case – in, out, open and close. When you see what skills and behaviours your toddler likes to practise, you can get creative and involve them with your everyday activities (just make sure the materials and items are safe for toddlers). Here are some ideas:

Behaviour	Play and toy ideas
Opening and closing	Jars with lids; old purses; containers with different openings; Tupperware containers
Putting in and taking out	Peg puzzles with large, chunky pieces; helping take laundry in and out of the basket or the machine; emptying a drawer of clothes and putting them back
Sorting and arranging	Sorting games with balls, figures or shapes; arranging cups in a row; matching socks
Exploring the senses	Books that let them explore textures; playing with water, flour, lentils or other sensorial materials in the kitchen
Striking	Banging on drums or triangles; banging on pots with wooden spoons and whisks (make sure you can handle some noise!)
Shaking	Ringing handheld bells; shaking maracas or keys; rattling bags of pasta

But how do I play?

It really feels like all Danes are naturally good at playing with kids. It's like they have a secret guidebook for speaking 'child'. This is probably because it's such a deep part of their societal DNA. After many years of working with parents and families, we have captured this guidebook for 'non-Danes' with the acronym MAP: mirror, ask, play. Here's how it works:

Mirror	Ask	Play (parallel play)
Start by sitting or lying beside your child and quietly observing what they are doing. Reflect back what you see. Don't overthink or adultify your dialogue.	Ask what they are doing and if you can join in.	Play quietly on your own next to them. Usually, kids will get curious and come and join in.
For example: • 'I see you are playing with your blocks. Those are nice colours you are building with.' • 'I see you are making dinner. It looks yummy.' • 'I see you are playing with your dolls. That looks fun.'	For example: • 'What are you building? Can I give you some blocks?' • 'What are you cooking? Can I help?' • 'What are you and the dolls doing? Can I play?'	For example: • Start building with your own blocks. • Begin to cook something in the play kitchen. • Pick up a doll and start brushing its hair. Kids will very often come and join you on their own.

Indoor play with young children (4–6)

Children love to play with other children

This is just a fact. So, while we, as adults, can be good play-mates, we can never give our children what other children can in terms of social skills, new challenges and fantasy. So whether it's siblings, friends or classmates, do prioritise time around other children.

Let them be bored

Don't be afraid of boredom. It's the birthplace of creativity. Even if a child says they're bored, be patient – they will soon come up with some form of play. Play is a child's way of processing new experiences, conflict and everyday events in their lives. You can learn a lot about your child's experiences and feelings just by tuning in and listening to them play.

Play and the common third

This is a concept that originated in social pedagogy and was developed by a Danish philosopher called Michael Husen. It describes how it is sometimes easier to talk with our children when we are taking part in a joint activity that we both enjoy. This is called the common third. Many of us have experienced how much easier it can be to talk with our kids when we are not face to face – for example, while on a walk, in the car, doing a puzzle, drawing or doing crafts. It's especially helpful for kids who have a harder time opening up.

🥾 'Talk is silver, silence is golden' 🥾

While 'common third' activities can be an excellent opportunity for some kids to open up and talk, we must be patient. Sit down and start drawing, painting or making beads at a table, and kids will almost always come to join you. Don't be afraid of the silence. When we say too much or fill the air with 'small talk', we interfere with the process going on inside the child's mind. Danish professionals say that 'talking is silver and silence is golden'. Kids who don't normally say much may suddenly start talking after a long time because their thoughts and emotions have had time and space to come out.

Be a playmate, not a prop

Parents are often told that we are *always* supposed to play what-ever the child wants to play ('Get into their world, follow their lead') and this can be boring for the parent and unrealistic for the child. Other children, for the most part, won't tolerate be-ing bossed around, so we aren't doing them any favours letting them decide everything. We also aren't including ourselves in any authentic way. If you play a game or take part in role play, try to do so through cooperation and negotiation.

Reading emotions

From early on, learning to read others' emotions is more im-portant than learning to read books in Denmark. Role-playing is a wonderful place to practise modelling empathy. Acting out storylines where you share things, soothe pain, handle conflict or talk about feelings will naturally develop thinking about others. Here are some ideas:

Role play idea	Social skills	Dialogue examples
Doctor/hospital: Going for a check-up or helping someone who is hurt. The child can examine you and ask questions as the 'doctor', or you can play through stuffed animals or dolls.	Soothing others: This is something we often overlook! When someone is sad or hurt, how can we soothe them? What can we say or do to help them?	• 'Oh no, your doll fell. Ouch, does that hurt? There, there, let me help you. Should we give her a hug?' • 'Is Bear afraid to go to the doctor? It can be scary sometimes – we understand you, Bear. But remember, the doctor is nice.'

Role play idea	Social skills	Dialogue examples
Tea party or picnic: Invite dolls, siblings or stuffed animals to tea or a picnic.	Learning manners: This is a chance to practise table manners and polite language away from the dinner table, which can be stressful.	• 'Could you please pass the milk? Thank you, that's very kind of you.' 'Bear, would you like a sandwich?' 'Wow, Bear that's a big bite. Remember to eat with your mouth closed.'
Restaurant: You can be the waiter or the customer. Create a menu together. Have a pad of paper and a pen for taking orders. These can be scribbled or drawn with pictures if your child can't write yet.	Being able to say no and ask questions politely: Practise asking and rejecting things politely, talking about likes and dislikes, and developing vocabulary around food and eating.	• 'Would you like to hear the specials?' 'No, I don't really like that.' • 'My soup is too cold!' • 'I'm sorry, but this isn't what I asked for.' • 'Could I please have some extra cheese?' • 'Do you like meat?'
School: Set up a classroom or lunch room with dolls or stuffed animals. You can be the teacher or the students. Set up social scenes from school to play out.	Handling conflict and modelling empathy: Practise talking about boundaries, conflict and inclusion, and pointing out how others feel.	• 'I see Clara, the new girl, wasn't included. Do you think she is sad? She looks a bit sad. Shall we invite her over?' • 'Let's talk to the others first before we tell the teacher. Maybe they don't know Clara is sad.'

Indoor play with older children (7–11)

The importance of touch

So many people grew up in 'colder' families where physical contact was not so normal. It can feel awkward for these parents to seek out contact with their children, but kids crave and need touch – and continue to do so as they get older!

Danes have massage classes in schools because it reduces bullying and creates more empathy. While we may not be ready for that, we can certainly seek out more opportunities for physical contact through play.

What's the difference between pure play and contest play?

Many sports and board games have the objective of defeating the opponent or winning. The older kids get, the more they will be involved in playing these kinds of games. The difference between pure play and contest play has a lot to do with our attitude to whether winning is tied to getting a reward or something external. It's good to be aware of these differences as parents. We want kids to know that winning and losing have nothing to do with being a good or bad person or receiving love from us.

Pure play	Contest play
When we want to strive for the fun of performing well (scoring, etc.) but don't keep score.	When the goal is to strive to win for trophies, grades, scholarships or other prizes.
When nobody cares who wins.	When we judge or measure ourselves by whether we win or lose.

When we keep score and strive to win, but just because it's a fun aspect of the game.	When there are spectators who will judge winners as the best and losers as the worst.

Pure play and contest play are both useful. There is nothing wrong with striving to win for rewards. Just be aware of how much importance you put on winning or being the best so your child's self-worth doesn't get caught up in it. Many sports have become so competitive that they're no longer fun. Schedule in time to play for the fun of it, and keep an eye on times when contest play seems to be edging out pure play.

Learning how to lose

This is a very important lesson, because it's the cornerstone of resilience. Losing and failing are part of life. It's perfectly normal to feel upset when we lose, but it's how we handle that pain that matters most. Some children need much more practice than others with losing, and playing board games or card games is a great way to get this.

HOW CAN I HELP MY CHILD LOSE WELL?

- **Don't tease them when they lose:** If your child is upset after losing, give them space.
- **Model being a good winner and loser:** Show that whether you win or lose, you really enjoyed playing the game and had fun.
- **Choose a cooperative game:** If your child really struggles with losing, try playing games where you can play together on the same team. This way, you can practise being good winners and losers together.

- **Reframe losing and use humour:** If your child plays badly and loses doing a sport, for example, you don't have to lie and say they played amazingly. Be honest, but try to use humour and lead them to more positive feelings. Acknowledge reality, eliminate the negative focus and build up the positive aspects instead. Practice makes perfect.

Child: 'I played so badly'

Parent: 'Did you break your leg?'

Child: 'No, but I am terrible at football.'

Parent: 'But you didn't break your leg? Are you sure?' *(feel both legs)* 'Well, at least you didn't break anything.'

Child: 'Ha ha. But I played so badly. I should quit. I hate it.'

Parent: 'Yes, you did play pretty badly today, but remember last week when you scored all those goals? Remember how you felt?'

Child: 'Oh yeah. Pretty good, I guess.'

Parent: 'You guess? I think you were dancing around singing, if I remember correctly. Did you hate football then?'

Child: 'No.'

Parent: 'Exactly. Now let's go have lunch and celebrate the fact that you didn't break your leg! I guess some games are good and some are bad.'

The power of *pyt*

There is a wonderful word in Danish: *pyt* (pronounced 'poot'), which essentially means 'never mind'. It's a way of discharging upset for smaller frustrations. A lot of schools have a *pyt* button kids can push – for example, if they are playing football and someone is getting really upset the coach may come around with the button and the kids can hit it and say, '*Pyt med det*' ('Never mind that', or 'We let it go'). Some schools hang the buttons on the walls. It's a way to acknowledge that it isn't nice to lose, but we can say never mind and focus on more positive things instead.

Try these ideas:

- **_Pyt_ button:** A button on a square piece of wood that your child can press and say, 'Never mind.'
- **_Pyt span_ (bucket):** Write down small grievances on paper, then crumple it up and throw it in the 'never mind' bucket.
- **_Pyt_ bracelet:** A string bracelet with a button on it. Kids can push it whenever they lose.

Note: *pyt* is not to be used for serious upsets. *Pyt* is really for little things we need to learn to be better at brushing off; it's not about dismissing your child's feelings.

Indoor play with tweens and teens (11–16)

Play starts to look different at this age

Play will change as your child grows up, but it still has the same core characteristics. It should be self-directed, self-motivated, governed by some rules and creative – and it should be something they can quit. It's good to keep this in mind as we balance between push and pull in their organised activities, homework and prioritising some downtime and hygge.

🥿 Know the difference between organised 🥿 activities and 'play'

Organised activities and play are different, but they are not mutually exclusive. Studying piano for an hour to practise skills is not the same as sitting down and experimenting with a new song by choice. A football training session with a coach is not the same as wanting to kick the ball around with friends. Ideally, as parents, we should aim to find a good balance between 'I want to practise and play because I like it' versus 'I have to practise because my parents are forcing me to.' If kids are able to tap in to their intrinsic playful drive at the same time as developing foundational skills, they can discover a passion for life.

When my daughter started playing piano in elementary school, she hated it. She went a few times, but then we stopped. A year or so later, I found a different teacher with whom she really clicked. She liked the lessons. She practised. We encouraged her, but backed off when it became unpleasant. After several years, she started experimenting with new songs, inventing her own songs and playing with friends. The piano was self-chosen, self-driven, had structure, was creative, and she could quit if she wanted to. If she hadn't developed the skills through lessons and practice, she wouldn't have had as much versatility to play freely. But she may not have wanted to play at all if she had always been 'forced' to practise. This is the delicate balance between 'I have to' and 'I want to'.

If lessons aren't working:

- Let them take time off if they hate it.
- Try a different teacher (this can make a tremendous difference, as I discovered in the example above). The relationship matters a lot.
- Try a different teaching method – every child learns differently.
- Try another activity.
- Back off and give them time to play, fail and innovate.

Identity

Tweens and teens try on different identities during these years, and define who they are through what they like ('I am a basket-ball player', 'I am into comic book drawing', 'I am a dancer', etc). These identities can be quite protective as they try to fit in. Having passions can help steer them away from the more challenging labels of 'I am a drinker', 'I am a partier' or 'I am a troublemaker'.

THEIR IDENTITY IS NOT ABOUT YOU

Remember that what they may like to do (or not do) isn't about how they represent you or your identity as a parent. Let's face it, most of our kids are not going to grow up to be professional athletes or musicians, but, if we are lucky, they may grow up to have a hobby that brings them great joy for the rest of their life. Some parents are so set on their child fulfilling their own unmet dreams that they never get to discover who their children really are, or how they express themselves creatively. Supporting your tween or teen in what they genuinely like is very important for their self-esteem.

They will have phases

Your tween or teen may suddenly stop playing the instrument or doing sports they were good at after many years. Sometimes it's OK to let them have a break and try something else. My daughter played piano beautifully for many years and then stopped suddenly and said she wanted to play violin. I was very frustrated, but after discussing it at length, I decided not to fight it but to go with it (the Danish Way). We agreed she could try a few lessons using a violin at school. Once I backed off and even set up the violin lessons, she completely went off the idea and went back to playing more piano than she had before. If it's a real interest, it usually comes back and it means so much more when it comes from them.

DON'T MAKE IT ABOUT THE MONEY

It can feel very frustrating when we invest in lessons or sports and our kids want to quit. You might find yourself thinking,

'We paid good money for that!' (this was one of my issues with my daughter quitting piano), however, if they genuinely don't like it, don't make it about the money. Things do change. That isn't to say money and commitment aren't important – they are! Make an agreement up front for how many lessons to start out with so they are a part of the decision. Some agreements could be:

- 'We agree you have to choose two activities – a sport and an instrument.' (Keep in mind that if kids are allowed to try out too many things, they won't take anything seriously.)
- 'You have decided to sign up for this, so you have to try it at least twice.' (Many places will allow you to do a free trial.)
- 'Once you have committed to this activity, you agree to follow through for x amount of time.'

There are some situations where kids may feel too over-whelmed, stressed, anxious or tired to keep up with their activities. Most experts in Denmark recommend listening to the child and respecting that they need a break.

Hygge: there is no 'I' in 'team'

This is perhaps the most important goal for parents of teens in Denmark when it comes to play. They want them to learn how to be part of a group or team *fællesskab* (community) and experience 'we', not 'I'. Many cultures are more individual-istic, wanting kids to strive to be the best, to be the winner. Danes focus much more on learning that 'we win together', and practising hygge is a big part of this. Even players of the most competitive sports prioritise spending a lot of time cosying around together. The belief is that when the group feels better, the individual feels better (not vice versa). You will hear things like:

'The team listens so well to each other.'
'They really take care of each other.'
'They are all so respectful of each other.'

Be ready!

While your teen may often say 'no' when you ask them to play a game, if they randomly kick a ball to you on a Thursday evening or want to play a game, drop everything and engage. There won't be many more opportunities for this, so we have to take them when they come!

Special days and rituals

Parenting pitfall:
Focusing on presents, not presence

Some of my fondest memories from childhood were when my mom put on her Christmas records and began to sing and decorate the house. I don't remember presents from that time, but I do remember listening to her happiness bubbling over, and it filled me with joy. Many Christmases later, after I'd had my first child, I was so intent on making the perfect 'experience' for our guests that I became frazzled and ended up in tears. It was a wake-up call. Looking back and remembering what had mattered most to me as a child, I wondered what had happened. It seems that in many cultures, 'special days' have become so commercialised that our internal compass has been unconsciously calibrated by marketing and social media. It creates a feeling of 'not enough', and takes the focus away from our own families. In Denmark, there is much less advertising in public spaces, and an intense value is placed on hygge, togetherness and wellbeing. Whatever holidays or special days you celebrate, this chapter is about creating a mindset based on what we know really makes a difference for genuine happiness: respect for presence. If you think this feeling doesn't matter for children, think again. It may be the most important gift we can give them.

PARENT tips

Play

Almost all special days in Denmark involve play with mixed ages. This is a huge part of the rituals and we highly recommend finding types of play that suit your family and making them a tradition. Board games, puzzles, crafts, ball games, cards – you choose! By associating these games with special days, especially if you start from when they are young, it will become natural for them to take part in the play as they grow. Scavenger hunts are very popular for birthday parties and can be done in groups or teams. Older children can be more responsible for younger ones, and adults can help encourage this by modelling inclusion of little ones in symbolic play. This could be letting them throw dice, move a counter on the board or toss a Frisbee with your help. The more everyone feels welcomed and involved in play, the more peace, joy and hygge there is overall.

Authenticity

Be true to yourself above all else and set boundaries around what matters to you. Many people get so caught up in the commercial pull of what holidays and special days are supposed to look like that they lose touch with what's really important. What are your values? What do you think your kids and family will remember in many years? Will they look back and think about the way things looked and all the gifts they received, or will they remember a feeling of harmony and happiness? Don't be afraid to say no to doing more if it sacrifices your ability to have peace. Holidays can also be times of grief and loss. It's OK to admit that everything isn't happy and perfect all the time. Allow space for joy, sorrow, gratitude, happiness, sadness and pain when they come. They are all welcome guests at the same table.

Reframe

Many families only see each other at certain times of the year, and it's so nice for kids to have positive experiences with less negativity and drama. Be ready to reframe hot-button issues and engrained family 'belief systems' that can be challenging around the holidays. Avoid black-and-white thinking like 'I hate this' and 'She always' or 'He never', and look for more nuanced and empathetic descriptions.

For example, perhaps you're thinking: 'I hate talking politics. I can't believe my parents think this way.'

Try to reframe as follows: 'My parents and I have different political views. We grew up very differently, and we are all living in social media silos these days. I don't like their politics, but I absolutely love them. Let's agree to not talk politics and focus on nice memories or stories we share rather than negative things that divide us. That is much nicer for everyone, especially the kids.'

Try making speeches on special days. This can be a wonderful way to build up the positive storyline for your child. Speeches and songs help strengthen the narrative you want them to remember. These speeches are a priceless gift that will be remembered forever and are great for adults too. I highly recommend trying it!

As well as reframing, I suggest you practise 'pre-framing' around special occasions. This offers you a way to visualise how you would like a family gathering to go and mentally prepare for it in advance. Instead of imagining the worst-case scenario, you focus on the best-case scenario and go over it in your mind.

For example: 'My mom is going to be stressed – so how can I help her rather than be annoyed? I'll bring a dish she needs, and I'll ask her what I can do to help, but I won't try and take over.'

Empathy

Check in with yourself so you can get what you need. If you are feeling anxious, run-down or frazzled, make sure to check in and have empathy for yourself, and take the steps you need to so you can get to a place of peace for your kids.

- **Are you feeling exhausted?** Ask for help and try to get some rest.
- **Are you feeling judged?** Remember you are your own worst critic, and your relationship with your children and partner matter most.
- **Are you feeling stressed over finances and what you may or may not be able to afford?** Remember it's the presence not presents that truly matters. Look for things that don't cost money but add priceless value.
- **Are family dynamics stressing you out?** Try to reframe.

No ultimatums

Holidays and special days can create power struggles because we feel uncomfortable, judged or stressed from the preparation involved. It's a time when meltdowns erupt from sheer exhaustion and sibling jealousy can rear its head. Practise empathising and understanding the meaning behind behaviour rather than shaming, blaming or punishing. Pass the baton to your partner if you need a break. Don't be afraid to default to movies or screentime, but try to make some media agreements in advance to avoid arguments. Remember that taking everything on yourself is a recipe for disaster, so don't hold back from asking for help to take the pressure off.

Togetherness and hygge

Holidays are the perfect time for hygge and adopting a team mentality. Everyone can have a role, and if you start young, tweens and teens still continue to look forward to baking cookies or helping out with rituals that have been part of their traditions growing up. The Hygge Oath (page 281) is to keep family dynamics harmonious at these times. It really works! Print it out. Read it. Talk about it. Discuss the 'tenets'. Put the Hygge Oath on the refrigerator so everyone can see it. If you can carve out a period of time to make a safe psychological space, the day will be so much nicer. Remember: 'When you replace the "I" with "we", even illness becomes wellness.'

Christmas in Denmark is probably one of the most hygge-filled periods that you will find at any time of year. Danes burn more candles than any other country in Europe. The cast of their golden glow can be found morning, noon and night. The spirit is not about consumerism, but natural simplicity, cosiness and togetherness.

Christmas hygge is all about the senses and the atmosphere. It's a mood. It's a feeling. It's a state of being. A great way to create hygge is to activate the five senses.

- **Sight:** hang decorations, put up a tree, watch festive movies, enjoy warm candlelight
- **Smell:** bake cookies, collect pine cones
- **Sound:** listen to Christmas music, sing songs, read aloud, enjoy a crackling fire
- **Touch:** cuddle up under cosy blankets, bask in the warmth of a fire, make homemade and natural decorations
- **Taste:** make hot chocolate, drink *gløgg* (similar to mulled wine), enjoy Christmas food, cookies and cake

🧦 What are rituals? 🧦

Rituals are regular intentional acts that bring a sense of meaning, identity and culture to a family. They become especially memorable around holidays and special days. They can be simple and inexpensive, but they have a profound impact.

Some examples are:

- decorating your home in a particular way, using the same items
- baking or cooking particular dishes
- the way you exchange gifts (see overleaf)
- making crafts together
- special music or songs you sing
- retelling uplifting stories from the past

Rituals are important because they:

- **Provide stability in stressful times:** Rituals and traditions help children feel more secure, especially during times of change or upheaval.
- **Create a sense of identity and belonging:** Rituals tells us, 'This is who we are. This is what we do in our family.'
- **Help pass down family values:** Rituals reinforce the message of what's important.
- **Help mark important milestones:** Rituals are used to mark holidays, birthdays, graduations and so on.

Special days and rituals with toddlers (0–3)

Baking

Baking is an essential part of any Danish holiday. It stimulates the memory bank for years to come. Anything you bake consistently on special days, whatever your culture, will be cherished well into their teens and beyond.

Opening presents with presence; teaching respect and patience

There are some unspoken rules around the way presents are handed out in Denmark. They are opened with care, one at a time. By taking turns, it helps kids focus on what they receive, and they naturally learn about appreciation and gratitude. This is a group effort that requires patience.

- **Everyone waits while the first person opens their gift:** That person is then responsible for getting the next gift. If it's a small child, a family member can help them.
- **Allow time for discovery:** The family takes plenty of time to let the gift receiver open the present and ask what it is. There isn't a mad rush to open the next one.
- **Point out how others feel:** 'Now, let's see Grandma open her gift. Can you see she's excited?'
- **Give a pre-gift:** Whether you open presents on Christmas Eve or Christmas Day, some kids are allowed to unwrap one present earlier in the day to play with. It can be really hard to wait all night (as Christmas can go on well past midnight).

MODELLING GRATITUDE

Forcing children to say thank you isn't so common in Denmark. While they do think it's important to teach kids social codes, they don't believe you should force a two-year-old to say thank you. Instead, they model gratitude. When kids learn to say thank you because they understand it, rather than parroting empty words on command, it has far more meaning.

- **Say thank you together:** This models how it's done. For example, 'Sophia and I thank you for the present,' or 'We thank you for the gift.' As kids generally want to cooperate with us, they will follow suit.
- **Be patient:** The more time a child is given to open a present and explore it with focus, the more they will naturally learn gratitude.

- **Don't reprimand them:** Shaming a child for not saying thank you can take all the warmth out of a joyful moment and can even be counterproductive. Be patient. They will get it.

DEALING WITH JEALOUSY

It is normal for kids to sometimes get jealous of each other. Jealousy is just a feeling, like all the others. There is nothing to be ashamed of. They will process it more quickly if they are allowed to feel it rather than being told they are wrong for feeling it.

Show your child you understand by saying: 'I can see you're sad your brother got that gift ... you would have liked one of those too.'

Acknowledge their feelings, then redirect: 'I can understand you feel jealous. Oh, I think I see another present under the tree that has your name on it. What's that?'

Special days and rituals with young children (4–6)

Be true to yourself

Marketers spend large amounts of money trying to make us buy in to an ideal of how special days should appear, leaving us feeling guilty and bereft for not reaching it. This is so subtle we don't even realise it, and it almost always involves buying things. Try to tune out the ads, social media and comparison, and ask yourself what really matters on these special days.

- **What are your genuine priorities for your family?** Is it more important that everything looks 'perfect', or that you are able to be calm and present?
- **How can you minimise stuff and maximise feelings of togetherness?** Is it more important that you buy more gifts, and 'do' more, or that you have more energy and time to be with your children/family?
- **What will they remember?** What will your children, your partner and your family look back on and remember most in many years' time?

Birthdays

Danish birthdays are very down to earth compared to birthdays in many other cultures. Schools often talk to parents to remind them to keep parties and birthday food simple so that everyone can feel good. It's not a competition.

This is what a Danish birthday might look like for a kid in this age group:

- **Start in the morning:** It's standard practice to wake up the birthday girl or boy with a song, and a tray holding a little cake or cupcake with a candle and a present or presents. This was really foreign to me in the beginning, but my kids absolutely love starting their birthday first thing in the morning. The party can continue later but this sets the tone for the day.
- **Parties are simple:** It's not about bouncy castles and fancy venues. There's more of a 1970s style, where the focus is on basic traditions, simple games and respect for the day.

- **Food and drinks:** Parents are reminded that it's nice for kids to just have a few things rather than many. Simple buns, cake, candy, chocolate milk, fizzy drinks or juice. Less choice means more focus on what's important, and it also means parents aren't left feeling like they aren't 'enough'. I am a little embarrassed to admit that we used instant cake mixes in my house, and still do today (decorated with candy). My kids love it. It became a tradition for us; simple, easy to make, 'homemade' – and everyone is happy.

Scavenger hunts

This is one of the most popular games to play at birthdays or kids' parties. There are many variations but it's usually a team activity, as kids love to run around together.

- **Have a starting point:** Place a note with a riddle to solve that leads the players to the next spot. It could be a little poem or clue that leads them to the tallest tree in the garden or beside the big rock. Once there, they will find another clue.
- **Use puzzles:** The clues they find at each spot might involve working out letters using arithmetic. For example, $3 + 3 = 6$, for the sixth letter of the alphabet: 'F'. In the end, the teams have to look at all the letters they find to spell out the code word 'FRIENDS'.
- **Make a physical map:** The players can read the map to find clues in the garden, woods, beach, countryside or park.

Ønske liste ('wish list')

Within families, any time a present is required for birthdays or special days, kids and adults alike are expected to produce a wish list for what they would like to receive – and it's taken very seriously. You get what you ask for. While this may sound a little boring, it's actually nice, because you always get what you want, and there's no unnecessary waste or money spent on useless stuff.

Small children are too little for wish lists so they get more presents. The focus is more on kids than adults. In big families at Christmas time, the adults often get one name each and just buy a gift for that person.

Natural decorations

There is less consumerism around buying decorations in Denmark, and much more focus on making them together. Anything you can make with nature is a cosy activity to enjoy over the holidays.

- Collect pine cones, then turn them into *nisse* ('gnomes') by gluing on cotton-wool hair and beards, and giving them buttons for eyes.
- Gather moss, lichen, twigs and acorns to make candle decorations and wreaths.
- Collect sticks and tie them into star shapes to hang up.

Making the whole period special

Whatever holidays you celebrate, embrace these wonderful opportunities to create your own rituals. In Denmark, the

Christmas mood starts from 1 December, and there are several ways they make the whole month matter.

- **_Kalederlys_ (calendar candle):** This candle has all the twenty-four days until Christmas marked on it, and is lit every day from 1 December, and allowed to burn down until it reaches the next day's date.
- **Gift calendars:** Every morning from 1 December, the child can open a very small gift (such as socks, chocolate or LEGO). These calendars make wake-ups and morning routines while school is in session _so_ much nicer and easier!
- **Christmas shows:** In Denmark, most families sit together to watch a specially made series throughout December called _Julekalendar._ Choose some classic Christmas shows, movies, cartoons and make it a tradition to put them on every year.

Special days and rituals with older children (7–10)

Julefred (Christmas peace)

There is an expression that's often shared when you are feeling stressed and frazzled as Christmas time approaches: _Lad julefreden sænke sig,_ or 'Now let Christmas peace sink in.' This peaceful Christmas feeling is like a psychological destination. There are so many things to do before the holidays, but _Julefred_ is that place when everything is ready and you can finally sit down, let go and truly enjoy the moment. _Julefred_ – allowing yourself time to sink into that feeling of peace – is a goal in itself.

Everyone plays a part

One of the main elements to hygge and getting to *Julefred* is that everyone has a part to play. Danes tend to know what to do (or look for what to do) because the interactive element of hygge is so engrained in them. Everyone helping is a huge part of reducing holiday stress.

Napkin folding

Many Danes are really into making interesting and elegantly folded napkins on special days, and kids generally enjoy being involved in this task from a very young age. They learn from aunts, parents or older kids, or watch tutorials. Children in this age group can absolutely do this on their own, and they really love it.

- Choose a napkin design together on YouTube or in a book.
- Help them fold the first one.
- Put them in charge of folding the napkins.
- Admire the work and creations, and encourage sibling involvement.

Make your own traditions

The holidays can be a lovely time to create a special activity you do together outside the house. As your kids get older, this can be a wonderful way to recapture the joy of past years. What can you choose as a special activity over the holidays?

- going ice skating together
- going bowling together
- planning a trip together for the New Year
- eating at a favourite restaurant

🧦Focus on 'we' 🧦

Remember, when you replace the 'I' with 'we', even illness becomes wellness. It doesn't matter what traditions you decide to create, just don't take everything on yourself. This is *not* hygge! Keep this mantra clear in your mind and repeat it often. It's a form of reframing, and the more you focus on it, the more it will happen. You will be so happy when your kids are older.

Danish traditions

MAKING DANISH CHRISTMAS HEARTS

The braided Christmas heart is a classic tradition, and you will see them literally everywhere in Denmark. They were invented by Hans Christian Andersen, one of the world's most famous fairy-tale authors, in 1873. They disappeared for forty years and came back in 1910 as part of the 'play' educational theory, because they teach children so many important skills and are good for all ages. There are lots of instructional videos online.

RISALAMANDE (CHRISTMAS RICE PUDDING)

This is a fun tradition that helps kids stay more present at dinner. It's essentially rice pudding with warm cherry sauce on top filled with small chopped-up almonds – and one whole one hiding in the mix. The fun part is that whoever finds the whole almond wins a special gift. It adds a sense of excitement for children throughout the meal in anticipation of dessert.

PAKKE LEG

This is a game which is good for older children and teens. It's also a favourite with adults at work parties. Here's how to play:

- Everyone brings three small presents based on an agreed budget.
- The presents are placed anonymously in the middle of the table so you don't know who put them in.
- Roll the dice. Whoever gets a six can take any present from the middle of the table.
- After all the presents are gone, set a timer (usually thirty minutes, depending on the number of people).
- Everyone keeps rolling, and whoever gets a six can steal whatever present they want from other people's piles. If you roll a one, you have to give a present away.
- Once the timer stops, you open and keep the presents in front of you.

Special days and rituals with tweens and teens (11–16)

Encourage older children to play with the younger ones

At Danish gatherings, it is really common to see kids of all ages mixing together. The older children begin to have more responsibility because they are the ones leading the play. This is usually learned through modelling over the years, but you can encourage it even if it's new for your family. This is so good for teens and young ones alike. As adults, you can lead the play by showing how to involve everyone, sending the message that this is how you play together as a family.

- **Put out toys, games, arts and crafts:** Choose things that can work for a mix of ages, like board games, ball games and so on.
- **Model inclusion:** If you are playing a board game, include small kids even if it's symbolic so they can feel a part of it. Let them hold a card or move a piece forward on the board.
- **Screens:** As long as kids are playing together, screen games can be OK. Just be sure to set and respect media boundaries and have plenty of non-screen play too.

Say it in a speech

Giving speeches for teens (and adults) is a huge tradition in Denmark, and it completely changed my approach to how I celebrate special days. Anyone can choose to give a speech. It's not mandatory, but very common. Speeches are often the most memorable part of any special day because they so beautifully highlight your child's value to you, which is the most priceless gift. They are usually delivered around a hygge table full of food and drinks or coffee and cakes. Speeches can be made for birthdays, confirmations, grad-uations, anniversaries or any special day. As an alternative to a speech, some families write a letter or poem they read out instead.

Here are some tips for speech-writing for special days.

Brainstorm stories and memories	Think of special memories, moments and experiences that describe your relationship with your child and their personality. Brainstorm with other family members or friends to help.
Talk from your heart	Don't think too much about it, just say what you feel. Think about who your child is and why they are so special. Remember to highlight who they are, not just what they've accomplished. Use words like: loving, curious, silly, funny, caring, thoughtful, brave, courageous, steady, etc.
Use humour	Choose some anecdotes that are funny but remember that it should be nice and light-hearted (not mean). Stories that everyone can laugh with, not at, are the key.
Practice makes perfect	Run through the speech in a mirror a few times beforehand. This will help a lot with timing, improving content and reducing nervousness.
Make eye contact	Pause, speak slowly and make eye contact with your child and the guests throughout the speech. This makes everyone feel more included.
Have a clear ending	Something like, 'And finally, I want to add . . .' or 'The last thing I want to mention is . . .'.
Always finish with a toast	'Can everyone please rise and raise a toast to (name). *Skål*! (cheers!)'

Sing it in a song

If you have seen any Danish movies, you have probably seen some group-singing taking place. Right along with speeches, Danes also love to make songs for special days. They take the tune to a popular song everyone knows and then add lyrics about the person's life or the special day – teens love it (well, most do when it's done well!). There are companies that will make songs for you (they also help with speeches). You just send them the personal information, and they make it into a song.

   Here are some tips for making your own song for a special day:

Choose a popular song to which everyone knows the tune	For example, 'Yellow Submarine' by the Beatles.
Create a funny storyline about the celebrated person or couple	Write out the main things you would like to say – it can be silly and funny.
Choose the number of verses and work out the number of syllables there should be in every line.	Fit the words to match the tune you've chosen, or it will be hard to sing. For example: 'When he was ten, he liked to play With funny friends from far away. When he was twelve, he changed his school, And all his friends thought he was cool.'
Print out the song lyrics to hand out to everyone so you can sing it together	Include some funny photos on the page next to the lyrics.

Discuss and try out the Hygge Oath

Hygge comes naturally to Danes because they grow up with it. It's a little more work for non-Danes, which is why the Hygge Oath can be such a helpful tool.

   Spend some time discussing what hygge is and get some consensus around it – it takes a team effort. Remember that we can complain at any other time, but for these moments, we agree to create a psychological oasis. The agreements include:

   no controversial discussions
   leave complaining and negativity outside
   turn off technology

tell and retell funny and uplifting stories from the past
enjoy the food and drinks
everyone helps out

You'll find the full Hygge Oath on page 281.

Baking

Parenting pitfall: The proof is in the pudding

When my daughter was little, I wanted to bake a special cake with her for her fifth birthday. We were having a party, and I chose a very fancy recipe I really wasn't comfortable making. I didn't consider myself 'a baker' at that time, so I felt nervous about getting it right. Looking back, I don't know who I wanted to get it right for. It seems like I was more focused on how my cake was going to look for the other parents at the party than I was on actually enjoying baking with my daughter. In the end, I shooed her out and made the cake by myself because I was too stressed to include her. It definitely wasn't a cosy time – and I ruined the cake and ended up buying one! The next year, I went back to using the instant cake mix she loved. We had a lot of fun making and decorating it together. I regretted letting the competition that sometimes exists in the parenting world dictate what I chose instead of focusing on what was really important – being with my daughter.

In Denmark, baking is a huge part of growing up. From a very young age, children bake at home and in schools. There are many television programmes that have been created for kids that encourage baking, sharing baked goods with loved ones and learning maths through the process. All schools in Denmark, from kindergarten onwards, have kitchens where children practise baking. It is considered a core element of 'hygge' at home – from easy bread-making to cookies and cakes. Research shows that baking fosters feelings of wellbeing, contributes to stress relief and can improve self-esteem and self-confidence. Just try it. Believe in it. The proof is in the pudding.

PARENT tips

Play

There is so much opportunity for play while baking, either together or in parallel play (such as drawing with flour, giving your child some dough to play with, or letting them have their own project like forming breakfast buns in a creative way).

Baking can be a fantastic way to play with maths. For younger kids, it could be counting the buns, while for older kids it can be learning the measurements, understanding fractions or even analysing recipes. Look for baking books aimed at smaller children with pictures to help them understand what is happening so they can follow along. The goal is not 'learning' per se, but there is a very natural exploration, experimentation and discovery process that happens through baking, which is more important than the outcome.

Authenticity

Keep it simple and keep it 'real'. Your kids don't need organic three-layer cupcakes with cocoa buttermilk frosting and fancy decorations. They really love just being with you – not a stressed-out version of you trying to attain some *MasterChef* ideal. Don't overcomplicate the process. Repeat simple recipes over and over again, like making buns, crêpes or pancakes. This isn't boring for children! It's how they gain confidence and independence and feel capable. It takes a lot of awareness to stay away from societal pressures to be 'the perfect parent', so check in with yourself often. Do what is comfortable and fun for you and your child; don't worry about the rest.

Reframing

If you find yourself saying, 'I am not a baker,' try to change that, because you are modelling for your kids and they may love to bake. Instead of saying, 'I am terrible at baking,' look for elements you do like, and say something like, 'I'm not fond of making cakes but I really enjoy making pancakes together on the weekends.'

Try to focus on all the benefits that baking offers. It's a kind of mindfulness. It reduces stress and gives you opportunities to strengthen your relationship with your child. This becomes especially nice in the tween and teen years, when they bake a cake for you or for others, and all that time you spent together in the kitchen comes back tenfold. It's also sweet to be able to conjure up good memories through the senses simply by baking.

Empathy

It's important to recognise the *lysten driver værket*: 'the desire that drives the work'. Baking rituals are generally appreciated from early on, especially to mark special days, but if your child doesn't have the desire to bake, there is no need to force it. Sometimes it comes later and sometimes it doesn't. We are all different.

See baking from your child's perspective, depending on their age. Toddler and pre-schoolers like to just be with you, and want to feel helpful and included. They also love experimenting with materials and textures. For older kids, pay attention to what they are interested in. Are they more health-conscious, or are they particularly interested in learning new recipes? Do they like a special kind of tea or brunch item that's in vogue? The more we understand what kids like to do and eat (genuinely), the more we can meet them where they are and be able to share the baking experience together.

No ultimatums

Many kindergartens and schools in Denmark recommend that children who have difficulties sitting still or concentrating train their sense of touch. The tactile sense helps with balance, stability, body sensation, body awareness and concentration ability – and baking helps train the tactile sense! As always, try to set up the baking scene so that you have the patience to handle mistakes and spills. Aim for fun, not perfection. Don't worry about the mess; it can easily be swept up afterwards. If you don't look for problems, you won't find them.

Togetherness and hygge

Baking is the embodiment of hygge: the smells, the tastes, the feeling. Baking appeals to all five senses and increases feel-good endorphins. It doesn't matter what you're making, just add hygge as the main ingredient in every step. Share the smiles, the curiosity, the exploration. Hear the laughter, the questions, the observations. Feel the dough, the peaceful playfulness, the togetherness. Taste the sweetness of the littlest things. The deliciousness of the now. It sounds so simple – and it is, in theory – but trust me when I say that hygge is the secret ingredient. If you pay attention to this, children will model it naturally, and this is the real recipe for success.

Baking with toddlers (0–3)

A classic Danish baking recipe

First, I am going to walk you through the process of baking one of the most classic and basic recipes that all Danish families make. These *boller* (buns) are generally enjoyed at breakfast with butter, jam or cheese. Children of all ages – including toddlers – can join in with making them.

Boller

Ingredients

100g butter
200ml milk, lukewarm
50g fresh yeast
2 eggs (1 for the dough, and 1 for glazing)
500g plain flour
50g sugar
1 teaspoon salt

Method

1. Melt the butter in a saucepan over a low heat, then take off the heat and pour into a bowl with the milk.
2. Add the yeast to the milk mixture (which must be luke-warm), and stir to dissolve.
3. Once dissolved, break 1 egg into the mixture and stir to combine.
4. In a separate bowl, combine the flour, sugar and salt.
5. Add most of the flour mixture to the wet mixture and beat until smooth.
6. Keep adding the rest of the flour mixture until you have a soft dough. Knead it until it doesn't stick to your fingers.
7. Let the dough rest in the bowl under a clean cloth for 20–30 minutes at room temperature.
8. Knead the dough again.
9. Cut and shape the dough into 12 big or 16 smaller slightly flat balls (see page 269 for some tips) and place them on a baking sheet. Cover with a clean cloth and leave to rise for about 15 minutes until doubled in size.
10. Beat the second egg in a bowl to make an egg wash, and brush this over the top of each bun (if you like, you can add a splash of milk to the egg wash).
11. Preheat the oven to 200°C (400°F/gas mark 6) and bake for 12–15 minutes until golden.

So, how can your toddler help you bake these buns?

As you follow the recipe above, try these ideas to include them.

SETTING OUT THE INGREDIENTS

Begin by putting all the ingredients on the counter so you are ready to bake. Include your child in getting the bowls and spoons and preparing for baking. Ask them:

'Can you take this bowl and put it there?'
'Can you put out the spoons?'

MIXING

Even a child who has recently learned to sit on the floor can stir flour. From about nine months or a year, children can participate in the mixing process. Let them feel the flour, and it is even OK to taste just a tiny bit of it. Children under three feel and experience by tasting or putting things into their mouth. It won't taste good, so they'll stop eating it on their own. Give them a spoon and a bowl so they can mix at the same time as you. That is more than enough to let them feel they are participating in the project, even if it is parallel play.

DISSOLVING THE YEAST

Remember, the milk has to be warm or the yeast will be killed. Toddlers can be responsible for dissolving the yeast with their hands in the milk. You can help by feeling it together. Try to make sure all the yeast is dissolved without sending the message that they are wrong or you are checking if they did it right. You could say: 'Can I feel it too? It feels funny and nice, right?'

BREAKING THE EGG

Toddlers may have a hard time breaking the egg, but you can try it in a separate bowl, and that way you don't need to use the egg with eggshells in it if they fail. Alternatively, you can pick out the shells together. At some point, they will succeed. Be patient. Breaking eggs is something most kids love learning how to do.

MIX THE DRY INGREDIENTS INTO THE WET MIXTURE

Pour in the dry ingredients slowly – not all at once – and stir to get rid of any lumps. Depending on your toddler's fine motor skills, let them (or help them) stir the dough with a big wooden spoon.

KNEADING THE DOUGH

Children of all ages can have fun touching the dough with their hands! Toddlers can have some of the dough to be responsible for (make sure they don't eat it). Let them play with it while you do the rest with a mixer or by hand. If you don't have a mixer, kneading the dough is a very good activity for kids of all ages to help with.

LETTING THE DOUGH RISE

Show your children that you are putting the dough aside to rise. It is also fun to see it once it has risen. Maybe they can set the timer and get a feeling of the period of waiting time. Say, 'Let's see how they look now. Do they seem bigger now?'

FORM THE BUNS

Give them some dough to play with while you cut and shape the rest of the dough into buns (see page 269) and place them on a baking sheet.

GLAZING THE BUNS

Your toddler can help with whisking the egg wash. Use a brush to glaze the buns. Place your hand around your child's hand and help them hold the brush and brush the mixture over the buns. If it's difficult, they can just try with some of them.

SETTING THE TABLE

When everything is ready, prepare for some hygge. Set the table and enjoy the buns with butter, jam and cheese, Danish style.

Baking with young children (4–6)

So, how can your young child help you bake?

Follow the *Boller* recipe on page 262, using these ideas to include your young child in the process.

SETTING UP THE SCENE

Make a little routine around 'baking time' so the set-up becomes part of the magic. Set out what you need to bake with on the table or counter. Ask your child for help finding the bowl, spoon, flour, eggs and so on from the kitchen cabinets.

You might say, 'Can you find the blue bowl we use for baking? Good, and do you remember what we measure the flour with? We need that one, too. Now, let's put all the things we need right here on the table, where we are going to make the dough.'

Get a foot stool or something for them to stand on. Turn on the oven together, then put on an apron (kids love having a little apron to wear for baking). Wash your hands, and you're ready to begin.

Try not to let concerns about tidiness take away from the experience. Expect a mess and prepare yourself mentally. You'll need to have patience and humour as spills and other small disasters occur.

MEASURING THE FLOUR

Older kids can read scales. With younger kids, they will enjoy using cups to measure. Show them where the flour should go, and let them spoon flour out of the bag and into the measuring cup. This could take some time, but let them try while you prepare something else. They will feel very accomplished when they are able to do this. A parallel play idea is to pour out a layer of flour on the table top and let them draw in it.

If they don't get the measure quite right, then be careful to adjust it without making them feel too corrected. Be understanding and share constructive guidance. You could say, 'It is not always easy to reach the exact spot, so I'll just take a little out again. You see? Now I think we have the right quantity of flour.'

MEASURING THE MILK AND DISSOLVING THE YEAST

If your child enjoys measuring, let them try measuring the milk too. The milk should be lukewarm, as if the yeast gets too hot or too cold, it will die and the dough won't rise. Explain to your child that when you touch the lukewarm milk, it should feel just the same temperature as your fingers. Dissolving the yeast into the lukewarm milk mixture is done with the hands, so it's a really tactile sensory experience.

Help your child understand when the yeast has dissolved properly: 'It's not always easy to dissolve the yeast. Here, let's feel again. There, now, can you see it's dissolved?'

MIX THE DRY INGREDIENTS INTO THE WET MIXTURE

Make sure your child sees that all the ingredients you have been working with are combined in one bowl. It will become clear that all the different things and processes you have been working on have ended up creating this dough. This is kind of magical and interesting for younger children to learn.

Depending on their motor skills, they can try stirring the dough until all the lumps are gone.

USE FLOUR WHEN KNEADING THE DOUGH TO AVOID STICKINESS

One of the tricks to kneading dough is to spread a lot of flour out on to the clean surface where you will knead it. This helps stop it from sticking to your hands. Young children will enjoy the fun of scattering the flour.

DIVIDE AND CUT THE DOUGH EQUALLY

This simple trick that Danes use may seem totally obvious, but it works wonders when trying to make the buns even-sized, and young children can help.

- Roll the kneaded dough back and forth until it forms a long sausage shape.
- Cut that 'sausage' of dough in half so you have two equal 'sausages'.
- Cut each of these lines in half so you have four even sections.
- Cut each of those in half so you have eight, and so on until you have the number of buns to form in the size you want. They will all be equal-sized this way.

FORMING THE BUNS

The standard way to shape the dough is to scatter some more flour over the surface, then roll each piece of dough under your hand in circular motions until it turns into a ball shape.

Young children will have more developed motor skills than toddlers, but it can still be difficult to form buns like adults do. This is part of the charm, because the buns can have many different forms and shapes. Perhaps they want to make something creative out of some of the dough while you shape the rest of the buns.

GLAZING THE BUNS

All children can be part of this. It's fun, and it also develops fine motor skills.

Baking with older children (7–10)

How to keep your older child involved

BAKE FOR BREAKFAST

Learning a new recipe with your child is a great way to bond. Every culture will have its own breakfast foods, but we recommend choosing something that can become a tradition in your family to enjoy at weekends or on special days. Choose a recipe that your kids can take part in. No matter what you choose, when hygge is the main ingredient, breakfast becomes a fond childhood memory. Some examples are:

- pancakes
- crêpes
- French toast
- bread or *bolle*
- cakes

LEARN A NEW RECIPE TOGETHER

Choose the recipe together, and let your child read it if they want to. You can 'analyse' what the text means, and decide which parts you will do together, but they can probably begin to measure, calculate volume or use scales on their own.

🦵 Baking with maths 🦵

Kids learn about maths naturally through experimenting in baking. This is tied to the concept of 'the zone of proximal development' or 'the sweet spot' of learning. This is when children are interested enough in what they are doing to keep trying because they feel challenged and curious to learn, but it's not so hard that they want to give up. Your role is to support or scaffold their learning just when they need it. Imagine your child is climbing over a log in a forest. You let them try to do it on their own. You give them a hand to help them if they need it, then just a finger, and then you let go when you know they can do it by themselves. You don't push them over or carry them over. This can be applied to any learning. In baking, as in any other process, we need to be aware of how much to help and when to stand back.

Remember this next time your child is:

- measuring
- weighing
- figuring out fractions
- looking up conversions
- doubling or halving the recipes

ENJOY BAKING SHOWS

These are very popular in Denmark, and usually consist of a beloved children's character baking together with kids, or teams who compete over many episodes. Baking shows are fun to watch together and can even give you ideas and inspiration for recipes to try.

Baking with tweens and teens (11–16)

Why should you keep baking with older kids?

Research shows that baking can create feelings of wellbeing, reduce stress and improve self-esteem and self-worth. It appeals to all five senses, which increases feel-good endorphins.

- **Baking stimulates the senses** of taste and smell, which can awaken happy memories and feelings of hygge.
- **Baking connects**. Sharing food with others activates our feelings of altruism.
- **Baking requires our full attention**; we need to be present with what we are doing. This act of mindfulness in the present moment reduces stress.
- **Better psychological functioning:** a study in the *Journal of Happiness* found that young adults who engage in activities like baking experience improved wellbeing in the form of better mood repair, social skills and the ability to be present.

How can I connect and get them more interested?

ENCOURAGE THEM BY HAVING AN ACCESSIBLE CABINET

For kids of this age, make sure that a 'baking' cabinet and tools are easily accessible so they can bake at will, especially if it has become a hobby. Having easy access to ingredients and their own cabinet means they can embark creatively on their own, with their friends during hang-outs or sleepovers, or with you. Believe it or not, when the ingredients are too high or difficult to find or reach, it can act as an impediment to them getting started.

OPT FOR WHAT THEY LIKE

What does your tween or teen like? Is there a new tea or coffee they are into, such as chai, matcha, bubble tea or cappuccino? Is there a trending breakfast food or cupcake or cookie they want to try? Did you enjoy a particular treat on a trip together that you could try and recreate? Teens start to like and explore new tastes, and you can always add this to the baking experience to capture their interest and show you are learning about their world.

Where do we go from here?

And so the question arises again. After more than forty years of being voted as one of the happiest countries in the world, what is it that has kept the Danes at the top of the happiness charts for so long? It is, in large part, down to the way they raise their children. Happy children grow up to be happy adults, and this is a cycle that repeats itself. You may have already been familiar with the concepts in this book having read *The Danish Way of Parenting*, or they may be completely new to you. *The Danish Way Every Day* illustrates how the PARENT framework can be practically applied to daily activities, routines and fun for all ages. It's a mindset and a philosophy. So the next time you think about what you have to *do* for your family – your blue script – you can think about how you want to *be* with your family, too – your green script. I am convinced that implementing even one or two tenets into your everyday lives will make a difference.

Here is a recap:

Play

Whether you're doing chores, cooking, going to bed or getting outside on a cold, rainy day, having a playful mindset can transform drudgery into joy and teach children some of the most important and essential life lessons: creativity, negotiation skills, critical thinking, resilience, empathy, self-control and so much more. Kids innately want to play, and they love being together with their parents. When you have the surplus energy, ask yourself: 'How can I infuse more playfulness into my everyday life?'

Authenticity

Honesty is the best policy. This means being honest with ourselves and our children about our moods, emotions, limitations and life in general – in an age-appropriate way. Getting caught up in a societal ideal of the 'perfect parent' prevents us from being able to rest well within ourselves – *at hvile i sig selv*. Kids don't need perfect parents, they need emotionally honest ones. Valuing humility, praising for effort rather than results, and nourishing the roots of self-esteem ('I am OK because of who I am') rather than the foliage of self-confidence ('I am OK only when I do or perform for others') yields more resilience, stability and wellbeing in the long run.

Reframing

When we see opportunities rather than obstacles – 'I get to' versus 'I have to' – we can transform our family life for the better. This includes reframing how we see cleaning, shopping, wake-ups and our children's digital lives, to name just a few things. This doesn't mean denying that negativity exists – not at all. It just means being better at seeing the positive details that always exist. It's about avoiding limiting labels for ourselves and our children, and building up the more positive storyline instead. And you get better with practice! When we actively focus our attention on the good stuff, the good stuff gets bigger, and ultimately becomes a self-fulfilling prophecy.

Empathy

Tuning in to our children and ourselves every day is so important. Look for the meaning behind their behaviour and help children understand that they have the right to their own feelings, senses and needs – this is fundamental to them learning how to trust in themselves and their 'gut' feeling. Being vulnerable and admitting when we are wrong are among the most connecting and empathetic things we can do. By avoiding shaming or judgement in general, being curious about others' perspectives and pointing out the good in others, we help set up our kids for deeper relationships and more happiness.

No ultimatums

Many parents believe that governing with fear and control is the most effective way, but fear fosters fear, while respect fosters closeness and trust. Children who are helped to understand rules and boundaries rather than fear them develop a much stronger sense of self-control, and ultimately grow up to be happier, more emotionally stable adults. By avoiding ultimatums and looking for 'win/win' rather than 'I win' solutions in everyday life, you set yourself up for a cycle of respect that will come back to you, especially in their teen years.

Togetherness and hygge

The family is a team, and the more we treat it as such, the more everyone feels valued and needed. Hygge is about carving out psychological space to connect with one another in our everyday lives. It's about prioritising 'we time', not 'me time', and it helps us appreciate each other in an oasis of cosiness. It's not mindfulness, it's 'we-fulness'. It takes effort and awareness to make hygge happen, but it's possibly one of the most important pillars of the Danish Way: by engaging in hygge, you sow the seeds for more happiness as a family. What a lovely legacy to pass on.

The PARENT philosophy may sound simple, and it is. But it's very often the simplest changes that can be the most profound. One day, we may all look back and realise that it was the small and simple things that were really the big and important things, after all.

APPENDICES

Hygge Oath

We agree to try to ...

Turn off the phones and the iPads.

Leave our drama at the door. There are other times to focus on our problems. Hygge is about creating a safe place to relax with others and leave the everyday stressors outside.

Not complain unnecessarily.

Look for where we can help out so that no one person gets stuck doing all the work.

Light candles if we are inside.

Make a conscious effort to enjoy the food and the drinks.

Not bring up controversial topics like politics. Anything that creates a fight or an argument is not hyggeligt. *We can have those discussions at other times.*

Tell and retell funny, lovely and uplifting stories about one another from the past.

Not brag too much. Bragging can be subtly divisive.

Not compete (think 'we' not 'me').

Not talk badly about others or focus on negativity too much.

Play games.

Make a conscious effort to feel gratitude for the people around us who love us.

Indoor play ideas

Toddlers (0–3)

Art and sensory play

- **Playdough:** Try rolling it flat, making a log, cutting it into small pieces and rolling it into balls.
- **Scissors:** Practise holding, opening and closing. Introduce cutting, starting with a sturdy piece of card.
- **Scribbling:** Give them soft, chunky pencils, wax crayons and toddler markers. Change the paper size, colour and texture. Let them learn how to use materials rather than worrying about how to draw.
- **Sensory play:** Enjoy sensory books and big wooden puzzles.
- **Bubbles:** A quick way to provide a lot of fascination.
- **Cardboard boxes:** These can become boats, houses, trains, caves ... If you have a decent-sized box, put it out and see what creativity happens.
- **Building blocks, Duplo, construction games, magnetic triangles, tool bench:** These provide endless opportunities for imaginative play.

Physical play

Note: Listen closely to any shrieks or screams and always check if they are for joy or in fear.

- **Airplane:** Pick them up and fly them around in the air like an airplane. This is a Danish favourite. You can also get some cuddles and giggles along the way.
- **Swinging:** Hold them by their arms and swing them in a circle, or toss them (gently) on to cushions.
- **Monster:** Take turns pretending to be a monster who is chasing the other person and planning to eat them for dinner.
- **Piggy-back rides:** You could also try going on your hands and knees, pretending to be a horse or a dog while they ride on your back.
- **Peekaboo and hide-and-seek:** Simply hiding under a cushion or blanket on the sofa is enough for toddlers.

Sing songs using the body

Using hand signals and clapping or making other sounds while singing facilitates learning and releases endorphins. Try:

- 'Heads, Shoulders, Knees and Toes'
- 'Incy Winsy Spider'
- 'The Wheels on the Bus'
- 'Old MacDonald'

Set up a play area

Try using:

- soft or rubber mats with puzzles or with designs to play on
- teepees or tents with strings of lights
- a swing to hang in the doorway

Young children (4–6)

Typical Danish toys and play areas

- play kitchen or restaurant area
- hygge place (a quiet nook with cushions, blankets and books)
- toy dinosaurs, dolls, plastic or wooden farm animals, puppets, stuffed animals, etc.
- toy trucks, cars, trains, construction vehicles, emergency vehicles, farm vehicles
- building blocks
- clothes basket or chest for playing dress-up
- arts and crafts area
- board games and puzzles
- balls and marbles
- hobby horse, hula-hoops, jump ropes, Twister (a good game for using your body)
- books, picture cards, puzzles

Physical play

OBSTACLE COURSES WITH CUSHIONS

All Danish play schools have a 'pillow room', which is just for kids to jump around in and be creative. Make an obstacle course out of cushions from the sofa and chairs or mattresses.

Try to set it up in a way that means you don't have to say 'no' or 'be careful' while they're playing.

THE FLOOR IS LAVA

Walk on cushions, towels or blocks (depending on your child's age). You can't touch the floor, because it's hot lava.

Arts and crafts

BEADS

There is no craft area or indoor play space in Danish schools without beads. Whether you're making bracelets, pictures, fabrics or designs, beads are a staple. Give your child boxes of beads in different sizes and colours, some twine or elastic, and some paper and glue, and let them create.

FINGER-KNITTING

This is an easy craft for ages five and up. You just need different coloured wool, your fingers and a simple video tutorial.

SEWING

Kids in this age group can learn sewing with a big, blunt embroidery needle (use a real one and trust them to use it). Give them some thread and a piece of cardboard with holes punched in it to pull the thread through.

MAKING A *HULE* ('CAVE')

Hule can be castles, houses, bear caves or forts; they can be indoor or outdoor. The only limit is your imagination.

For indoor caves, you can use tables and chairs covered with sheets or blankets, or big cardboard boxes. Fill them with cushions and pillows, add some string lights, and bring in some stuffed animals and books. Have a snack inside the *hule* and talk together.

Older children (7–10)

Physical play ideas

HAIR-BRAIDING

Many animals use grooming (essentially doing each other's hair) as a way to calm each other and express love. Get a book or look online for tutorials. It's a very nice way to be close and physically connect.

TAG, ROUGH-AND-TUMBLE OR PILLOW FIGHTS

All animals 'play' fight. Just like puppies or bear cubs, many kids need to roll around and wrestle. It is one of the most natural ways to burn off aggression, and can help reduce angry outbursts and conflict. Try to find spaces where you can be free to hurl pillows and wrestle for fun without worrying about something being broken. Make sure to share some cuddles and hugs at the same time.

SPA DAY

Set up a cosy home spa scene. Cut up cucumbers to put on the eyes. Mash avocado for a face mask (or use store-bought masks). Take turns lying down and massaging each other's heads, hands or feet. Light candles and play relaxing music. Don't think this is just for girls! Boys love this too.

Arts and crafts

HAMA BEADS

Like LEGO, HAMA beads are a Danish invention. These small plastic beads can be arranged on a pegboard to form a design, and then, using an iron and wax paper, you melt the beads together. When they cool off, you have a solid piece of plastic in your design.

PAPER CRAFTS

- **Paper folding**
- **Paper cutting:** Inspired by the Danish children's author Hans Christian Andersen, and popular since the 1800s. The different ways you fold and cut the paper reveals beautiful patterns. You will find these designs hanging in many gift shops today. This is a fun activity for older kids and teens.
- **Flip-flapper:** A folded paper game where you write questions and then, based on numbers or letters, you flip-flap the paper to reveal the answers.
- **Paper airplanes**
- **Origami**

Other play ideas

yo-yos

juggling

Rubik's cube

unicycling

making something out of a cardboard box

Twister

dancing to favourite songs

puzzle books

hangman

friendship bracelets

Tweens and teens (11–16)

IDEAS FOR PLAY TO SUGGEST FOR TWEENS AND TEENS

- playing cards, puzzles or board games
- ball games
- manicures or make-up
- watching a TV series or a movie
- making jewellery
- building a model airplane or LEGO model
- playing a video game
- baking
- going to a concert, the theatre, a sports game or an exhibition
- playing ping-pong, billiards or table football

References

Introduction

'I saw that Denmark had been voted the happiest country in the world by the OECD (Organisation for Economic Co-operation and Development).' The OECD Better Life Index measures the wellbeing of different countries. OECD, www.oecd.org

'. . . our book *The Danish Way of Parenting* . . .' Alexander, Jessica Joelle and Sandahl, Iben. *The Danish Way of Parenting: What the Happiest People in the World Know about Raising Confident, Capable Kids.* TarcherPerigee, 2016.

'Play has been considered an educational theory in Denmark since 1871.' BUPL. 'Historika tema; Før 1930'. bupl.dk. (https://bupl.dk/boern-unge/find-artikler/historisk-tema-foer-1930)

Dahl, Karen Margrethe and Ottosen, Mai Heidi. 'Kortlægnin af viden om opdragelse' ('Mapping knowledge about education'). VIVE (the Danish Centre for Social Science Research). vive.dk. (https://www.vive.dk/da/udgivelser/kortlaegning-af-viden-om-opdragelse-yxd452xg/)

For more inspiration on mindset, see: Tsabary, Shefali. *The Conscious Parent: Transforming Ourselves, Empowering Our Children.* Namaste Publishing, 2010.

Everyday activities

'In a Harvard Grant study that is one of the longest-running longitudinal
      studies in history (spanning seventy-five years from 1930 to the
      present) researchers uncovered two things that people need in order
      to be successful.' Murphy Jr, Bill 'Kids who do chores are more
      successful adults.' Inc.com, 29 March 2017. (https://www.inc.com/
      bill-murphy-jr/kids-who-do-chores-are-more-successful-adults-
      according-to-science.html)

CHORES

'According to the Center for Parenting Education, children who regularly
      do chores are better able to deal with frustration and delayed
      gratification, have higher self-esteem and are more responsible than
      those who don't do chores.' The Center for Parenting Education.
      'Part I: Benefits of Chores'. centerforparentingeducation.org.
      (https://centerforparentingeducation.org/library-of-articles/
      responsibility-and-chores/part-i- benefits-of-chores/)
'Play, by definition, is something you are always free to quit.' Gray, Peter.
      '#24: When Work Is Play'. petergray.substack.com, 3 December
      2023. (https://petergray.substack.com/p/24-when-work-is-play)
'Studies show that toddlers naturally help out when they see an adult in
      need of assistance.' Meltzoff, A.N. 'Understanding the Intentions
      of Others: Re-Enactment of Intended Acts by 18-Month-Old
      Children'. *Dev Psychol.* 31(5):838–850. September 1995.
' . . . the child feeling like a useful contributing part of the *fællesskab* (family
      community).' Alexander, Jessica Joelle and Andersson, Camilla
      Semlov. 'Fæellesskab and Belonging'. Othering and Belonging
      Institute, 15 February 2022. (https://belonging.berkeley.edu/
      democracy-belonging-forum/papers/faellesskab)
Carboni, Maj. 'Disse pligter har andres børn' ('Other people's children

have these duties'). Skolebørn, 2018. (http://skoleborn.dk/feb_2018/disse-pligter-har-andres-beorn.html)

Münster, Sophie. 'Tre enkle familievaner, der giver hjælpsomme børn' ('Three simple habits that produce helpful children'. nordicparenting.dk. (https://nordicparenting.dk/du-gerne-have-boernene-hjaelpe-uden-brok-noel-proev-goere-stedet-spoerge/)

Rende, Richard. 'The developmental significance of chores: Then and now'. *The Brown University Child and Adolescent Behavior Letter.* 31(1):1–7. January 2015.

SHOPPING

Juul, Jesper. *Din Kompetente familie.* Folaget Aprostof, 2008.

Juul, Jesper. *Livet i familien: De vigtigste værdier for at leve sammen og opdrage børn.* AuthorHouse, 2013.

For more inspiration on respectful discipline, see:

Lapointe, V. *Discipline Without Damage: How to Get Your Kids to Behave Without Messing Them Up.* LifeTree Media Ltd, 2015.

Ockwell-Smith, S. *Positive Discipline: The Calm, Practical, Everyday Guide to Parenting from Birth to Seven Years.* Piatkus, 2017.

COOKING

'Studies show that the more kids play with food from a very young age – especially while cooking – the more likely they will be to taste and enjoy what they eat.' De Montfort University. 'Children who play with food more likely to eat fruit and veg, researchers find'. dmc. ac.uk, 20 February 2017. (https://www.dmu.ac.uk/about-dmu/news/2017/february/children-who-play-with-food-more-likely-to-eat-fruit-and-veg-researchers-find.aspx)

'Studies show that the more children experience food through the senses, the more willing they are to taste it.' Københavns Kommune/

Børne og Ungdomsforvaltningen. 'SANSER & SMAGE' ('Senses and Tastes'). bornemenuen.kk.dk, 2023. (https://bornemenuen. kk.dk/sites/default/files/2023-11/Sanser%20og%20smage%20 undervisningsmateriale1.pdf)

'Studies have shown that kids who learn to cook from an early age have an advantage when it comes to language skills and basic maths skills.' Jo, Seungjung, and Son, Ji-Won. '"I Can Create and Eat it for Snack": How Can Cooking Activities Support Early Math Learning?' *Early Childhood Education Journal*. 50(4). 2022.

Sepp, H., and Höijer, K. 'Food as a tool for learning in everyday activities at preschool – an exploratory study from Sweden'. *Food Nutr Res*. 60(1). October 2016.

Health Food Choices in Schools. 'Cooking with Kids in Schools: Why it is Important'. healthy-food-choices-in-schools.extension.org, 21 June 2019. (https://healthy-food-choices-in-schools.extension.org/ cooking-with-kids-in-schools-why-it-is-important/)

Cunningham-Sabo, Leslie, and Lohse, Barbara. 'Cooking with Kids Positively Affects Fourth Graders' Vegetable Preferences and Attitudes and Self-Efficacy for Food and Cooking'. *Childhood Obesity*. 9, 549–56. 2013.

Science Daily. 'Adolescents' cooking skills strongly predict future nutritional wellbeing'. sciencedaily.com, 17 April 2018. (https:// www.sciencedaily.com/releases/2018/04/180417181125.htm)

EATING

' . . . the idea that the feeling of togetherness could be just as important as the food itself.' Madkulturen. 'Madkultur 2017: Sadan spiser danskerne' ('Food culture 2017: This is how the Danes eat'). madkulturen.dk, 23 January 2018. (https://www.madkulturen. dk/madindeks-2017-saadan-spiser-danskerne/)

' … studies show that kids might need to try a new food up to fifteen
      times before they like it.' Knudstrip, Amalie Hald. 'Gør op med
      kræsenhed' ('Do away with pickiness'). dr.dk, 22 February 2018.
      (https://www.dr.dk/mad/artikel/goer-op-med-kraesenhed-drop-
      madbeloenninger-og-vaer-et-godt-forbillede)

'If we respect our children regarding their senses, feelings
      and needs . . .' Jesper, Juul. *Din Kompetente familie*. Folaget
      Aprostof, 2008.

'All kids pass through picky eating "phases". This is totally
      normal.' Hansen, Helen Lyng. 'Leger med maden' ('Playing
      with food'). netsundhedsplejersle.dk, 23 November 2016.
      (https://www.netsundhedsplejerske.dk/artikler/index.
      php?option=laes&type=ARTIKLER&id=493)

'In a Canadian study (the first of its kind), researchers followed children
      from the age of five months up to ten years to see what effect
      eating together had on them in the long term.' Science Daily.
      'Eating together as a family helps children feel better physically
      and mentally'. sciencedaily.com, 14 December 2017. (https://www.
      sciencedaily.com/releases/2017/12/171214092322.htm)

See also: Sánchez, Edith. '10 fordele ved at spise sammen som familie
      ifølge videnskaben' ('10 benefits of eating together as a family
      according to science'). bedrlivsstil.dk, 9 August 2022.
      (https://bedrelivsstil.dk/fordele-spise-sammen-som-familie-ifoelge-
      videnskaben/)

'American kindergarteners who watched TV during dinnertimes
      were more likely to be overweight by the time they were in
      third grade.' Fishel, Ann. 'Science says: Eat with your kids'.
      theconversation.com, 9 January 2015. (https://theconversation.com/
      science-says-eat-with-your-kids-34573)

'In a recent survey, American teens were asked when they would
      most like to talk with their parents, and "at dinnertime"
      was their top answer.' Mann, Mirele. '9 scientifically

proven reasons to eat dinner as a family'. goodnet.
org, 5 May 2016. (https://www.goodnet.org/articles/
9-scientifically-proven-reasons-to-eat-dinner-as-family)

For more inspiration on connection, food and caring for your kids, see:

MacNamara, D. *Nourished: A Guide to Living in Connection with Your Child's Brain*. Empowering Education, 2020.

Routines

BUPL. 'Rutiner og hverdagspædagogik' ('Routines and everyday pedagogy').vbupl.dk. (https://bupl.dk/paedagogik-og-profession/forskningsunivers/rutiner-og-hverdagspaedagogik)

MORNINGS

'Psychologists have found that families who develop flexible routines that adapt to kids' developmental phases are less stressed.' Blackwell, S., Zylberberg, A., Scerif, G., Miller, S., and Woodcock, K.A. 'Understanding the psycho-social context for a new early intervention for resistance to change that aims to strike a beneficial balance between structure and flexibility'. *BMC Psychiatry.* 21(1):621, December 2021.

'They say seventy-five per cent of the time you'll get to spend with your kids is over by the time they turn twelve.' Yurich, Ginny. '75% of the time we spend with our kids in our lifetime will be spent by age 12'. 1000hoursoutside.com (https://www.1000hoursoutside.com/blog/time-with-kids-before-age-12)

For more inspiration on routines and peaceful parenting, see:

Markham, L. *Peaceful Parent, Happy Kids: How to stop yelling and start connecting*. Perigee, 2012.

AFTERNOONS

Christensen, Kristoffer Wulf. 'Bliv en mere nærvæ – rende forælder' ('Become a more present parent'). dr.dk, 6 February 2014. (https://www.dr.dk/levnu/boern/bliv-en-mere-naervaerende-foraelder)

Kristensen, Kim. 'Søvnmønster hos børn under 3 ar' ('Sleep patterns in children under 3 years of age'). sundhed.dk, 30 March 2022. (https://www.sundhed.dk/borger/patienthaandbogen/boern/sygdomme/oevrige-sygdomme/soevnmoenster-hos-boern-under-3-aar/)

'If you are too exhausted to engage much with your child, try the ten-minute rule.' Faerregaard, Birgitte. 'De Utrolige Ar' ('The Incredible Years'). sbst.dk. (https://www.sbst.dk/tvaergaende-omrader/virksomme-indsatser/dokumenterede-metoder-boern-og-unge/om-virksomme-indsatser-til-boern-og-unge/de-utrolige-aar)

'Interestingly enough, according to a study of different nationalities, Danish babies cry less than babies in other countries.' Siddique, Haroon. 'Babies in Britain, Canada and Italy cry more than elsewhere – study'. *Guardian*, 3 April 2017.

'Experts believe it takes at least five positive interactions to every negative one to keep a relationship strong.' Gonsalves, Kelly. 'This magic 5:1 ratio is the key to healthy relationships, marriage experts say'. mindbodygreen.com, 12 June 2022. (https://www.mindbodygreen.com/articles/magic-ratio-in-relationships)

See also: Dieter *et al.*, 'Systematic review and meta-analysis: Fussing and crying durations and prevalence of colic in infants'. *Journal of Pediatrics*. 185: 55–61, June 2017.

'... Danish recommendations for making it a "good pick-up".' Børns Vilkår. 'Den gode afhentning af dit narn I daginstitution' ('The good pick-up of your child at daycare'). bornsvilkar.dk. (https://bornsvilkar.dk/smaaboern/dagtilbud/den-gode-afhentning/)

'The fundamental attribution error.' Wikipedia. 'Fundamental
     attribution error'. Wikipedia.org. (https://en.wikipedia.org/wiki/
     Fundamental_attribution_error)

EVENINGS

'We, as parents, have more power than our children. Therefore, we must take
     responsibility for *how* we use that power.' Juul, J. *Family Life: The Most
     Important Values for Living Together and Raising Children.* AuthorHouse, 2012.
'This is the crux of equal dignity.' Juul, J., and Jensen, H. *Relational
     Competence: Towards a New Culture of Education.* Edition + Plus, 2017.
'*Karius and Baktus*: the Danish book that gets kids to brush their teeth!'
     Egner, T. *Karius og Baktus.* 1949.
'Growing research shows that assigning hours of homework to younger
     children has very little benefit for them.' Goodwin, Cara. 'Is
     homework good for kids?' pyschologytoday.com, 3 October 2023.
     (https://www.psychologytoday.com/intl/blog/parenting-translator/
     202309/is-homework-good-for-kids)
For more on homework and making homework agreements, see:
Mygind, Liv. '6 gode rad, der kan motivere dit barn til at lave lektier'
     (6 good tips that can motivate your child to do homework').
     samvirke.dk, 5 December 2015. (https://samvirke.dk/artikler/
     6-gode-raad-der-kan-motivere-dit-barn-til-at-lave-lektier)
Tonsberg, Signe. 'Der er læring I lektier – men nogle lærer mere end
     andre' ('There is learning in homework – but some learn more
     than others'). dpu.ad.uk, June 2022. (https://dpu.au.dk/asterisk/
     der-er-laering-i-lektier-men-nogle-laerer-mere-end-andre)
Palme Olesen, Emilie. 'Lektier er ikke den bedste vej til mere læring'
     ('Homework is not the best route to learning'. folkeskloen.dk,
     16 February 2023 (https://www.folkeskolen.dk/folkeskolen-
     nr-03-2023-forskning-kobenhavns-professionshojskole/
     lektier-er-ikke-den-bedste-vej-til-mere-laering/4700466)

BEDTIME

' . . . recommendations from the Danish National Health Authority for
    how much sleep kids need.' Lindhart, Christina Louise. 'Babyer og
    søvn' ('Babies and sleep'). sundhed.dk (https://www.sundhed.dk/
    borger/patienthaandbogen/boern/om-boern/det-nyfoedte-barn/
    babyer-og-soevn/)

'Research also shows that singing and rhyming develops children's
    language skills and speaking ability . . .' Goodyear, Charis.
    'Babies learn language best through sing-song speech, not
    phonetics'. neurosciencenews.com, 1 December 2023. (https://
    neurosciencenews.com/language-learning-neurodevelopment-
    25297/ https://www.bambinomio.co.uk/blogs/baby/
    the-role-of-nursery-rhymes-in-language-development)

'The Danish Health Authority recommends that the safest place for a
    small child to sleep is in their own bed in the same room as the
    parents.' Lindhart, Christina Louise. 'Babyer og søvn' ('Babies
    and sleep'). sundhed.dk (https://www.sundhed.dk/borger/
    patienthaandbogen/boern/om-boern/det-nyfoedte-barn/babyer-
    og-soevn/)

For more on sleep and babies, see:

Kirshenbaum, G. *The Nurture Revolution: Understand and Grow Your Child's
    Brain with the Science of Connected Parenting.* Penguin Life, 2021.

'A recent study conducted by Ohio State University found that young
    children who were read five books a day entered kindergarten
    having heard 1.4 million words more than kids who were never read
    to.' Grabmeier, Jeff. 'A "million-word gap" for children who aren't
    read to at home'. sciencedaily.com, 4 April 2019. (https://www.
    sciencedaily.com/releases/2019/04/190404074947.htm)

'Reading all kinds of stories builds empathy.' McKearney, Miranda, and
    Mears, Sarah. 'Lost for words? How reading can teach children
    empathy'. *Guardian*, 13 May 2015.

' . . . studies show that reading stories that feature a range of different emotions builds empathy and resilience.' Tackett, R. M. J., and Moore, C. 'Exposure to Media and Theory-of-Mind Development in Pre-Schoolers'. *Cognitive Development* 25(1): 69–79, 2010.

'From puberty to the age of twenty-two, teens need about nine hours of sleep a night.' Garey, Juliann. 'Why are teenagers so sleep-deprived?' childmind.org, 8 November 2023. (https://childmind.org/article/teenagers-sleep-deprived/)

'Research shows that parental expectations really do help kids make a commitment to changing their sleep patterns.' Dolan, E. 'Parent-set bedtimes result in healthier sleep patterns for adolescents, study finds.' psypost.org. 26 July 2023. (https://www.psypost.org/parent-set-bedtimes-result-in-healthier-sleep-patterns-for-adolescents-study-finds/)

Fun

For more on self-confidence versus self-esteem, see:
Juul, Jesper. *Din Kompetente familie*. Folaget Aprostof, 2008.

NATURE

Skoletid. 'Den Positive Indflydelse af Naturen på Børns Læring og Trivsel' ('The positive influence of nature on children's learning and wellbeing'). skoletid.nu.
    (https://www.skoletid.nu/hvilken-positiv-indflydelse-har-naturen-paa-boerns-laering-og-trivsel/)

Ejby-Ernst, Niels. 'Nature makes children happy – they say so themselves'. dn.dk, 30 January 2018. (https://www.dn.dk/nyheder/naturen-gor-born-glade-det-siger-de-selv/)

Center for Børn og Natur: https://centerforboernognatur.dk/projekter/kom-med-ud/

'Overwhelming studies show that small children get a host of
        benefits from going barefoot . . .' 'Frie fødder – mærk nature
        med dine fødder' ('Free feet – feel nature with your feet').
        groennespirer.dk. (https://groennespirer.dk/naturaktiviteter/
        frie-foedder-maerk-naturen-med-dine-foedder)
See also: Pedersen, Amalie, Jacobsen, Maiken, and Larsen, Camilla.
        'Sansning med bare tæer' ('Sensation with bare toes'). kpvalgfri.nu,
        9 October 2020. (http://kpvalgfri.nu/sansning-med-bare-taeer/)
'Kids who play in dirt are less likely to get sick because it strengthens their
        immunity, and some studies suggest that mud has antidepressant
        qualities that release serotonin.' Iftikhar, Noreen. 'Mud play for
        kids: Why it's worth the mess'. healthline.com, 21 December 2020.
        (https://www.healthline.com/health/childrens-health/mud-play)
See also: Franco, Alessia, and Robson, David. 'How mud boosts your
        immune system'. bbc.com, 11 October 2022 (https://www.bbc.com/
        future/article/20220929-how-outdoor-play-boosts-kids-immune-systems)
Raising Children. 'Noticing nature walk: activity for children
        3–8 years'. raisingchildren.net.au. (https://raisingchildren.
        net.au/guides/activity-guides/out-and-about/
        noticing-nature-walk-activity-for-children-3-6-years)
'Life, death and the mysteries of existence.' Naturguide. 'The youngest
        explore life and death in nature.' naturguide.dk (https://naturguide.
        dk/krible-krable-2022-de-yngste-udforsker-liv-og-doed-i-naturen/)
'Enjoying risky play in nature is important for your child's development.'
        Spencer, et al. 'Early childhood educator perceptions of risky play in
        an outdoor loose parts intervention'. AIMS Public Health. 8(2):213–
        228, March 2021.
'Six categories of risky play that children can benefit from . . .' Sandseter,
        Ellen Beate Hansen. 'Children's Risky Play in Early Childhood
        Education and Care'. ChildLinks. 3, 2011.
'Notice how . . . those rocks are slippery /the log is rotten/that branch is
        strong.' Bergeron, Josée. 'Stop telling kids to "Be careful", and what

to say instead'. backwoodsmama.com, 6 February 2018. (https://
www.backwoodsmama.com/2018/02/stop-telling-kids-be-careful-
and-what-to-say-instead.html)

'The benefits of nature.' Weir, Kirsten, 'Nurtured by nature'. *Monitor on
Psychology*. 51(3): 50. April 2020.

'Nature therapy.' Brath, Cathrine. 'Friluftsterapi: Naturen som kur
mod stress og angst' ('Outdoor therapy: nature as a cure for stress
and anxiety'). psykologidanmark.dk, 29 December 2022. (https://
psykologeridanmark.dk/2017/08/naturen-kur-stress-angst-ikke-
redigeret/)

For more on encouraging kids to enjoy nature, see:

Weinkouff-Hansen, Jacob. 'Danske børn vil gerne ud i naturen' ('Danish
children want to go out into nature'). kristelight-dagblad.dk, 16
September 2022. (https://www.kristeligt-dagblad.dk/danmark/
danske-boern-vil-gerne-ud-i-naturen)

Grundtvig, Annemette. '10 gode råd: Sådan får du børnene med ud
at gå tur' ('10 good tips: How to get the children out for a walk').
politiken.dk, 26 October 2014.
　　(https://politiken.dk/danmark/forbrug/livsstil/art5549446/
　　10-gode-r%C3%A5d-S%C3%A5dan-f%C3%A5r-du-
　　b%C3%B8rnene-med-ud-at-g%C3%A5-tur)

Louv, R. *Last Child in the Woods: Saving our children from nature-deficit disorder*.
Algonquin Books, 2008.

SCREENTIME

'Denmark is voted as having some of the highest levels of digital
wellbeing in the world . . .' Surfshark. 'Which country has
the best digital wellbeing in 2023?' visualcapitalist.com, 18
December 2023.
　　(https://www.visualcapitalist.com/cp/which-country-has-the-
　　best-digital-well-being-in-2023/)

See also: Wenande, Christian. 'Denmark ranked first for digital quality of
      life'. cphpost.dk, 15 September 2021 (https://cphpost.dk/2021-09-
      15/news/denmark-ranked-first-for-digital-quality-of-life/)

'It is recommended by the Danish Ministry of Health that kids under
      two years old don't use screens except to communicate with
      grandparents.' Børns Vilkår. 'Skærmbrug for børn 0–2 ar'
      ('Recommendations for 0–2-year-olds'). bornsvilkar.dk. (https://
      bornsvilkar.dk/skaermguiden/0-2-aar/#2-ar)

For more on screentime, see: Børns Vilkår. 'Skærmguiden' ('Screen
      wizard)'. bornsvilkar.dk. (https://bornsvilkar.dk/skaermguiden/)

Sundhedsstyrelsen. 'Har I styr pa skærmen I jeres familie?' ('Do you have
      control over the screen in your family?'). sst.dk. (https://www.sst.dk/
      da/styrpaaskaerm)

Shapiro, J. (2018). *The new childhood: Raising kids to thrive in a connected world.*
      TarcherPerigee.

Shapiro, J. (2018, March 10). *Parenting for the future: The new
      childhood* [Video]. TEDx Talks. https://www.youtube.com/
      watch?v=dQDHEejnn5U&ab_channel=TEDxTalks

Etchells, P. (2024). *Unlocked: The real science of screen time (and how to spend it
      better).* Bloomsbury Publishing.

Larsen, M. C., & Johansen, S. L. (2024). *Social media across everyday contexts:
      Digital childhood and youth in the Nordics.* Routledge.

Raising Digital Citizens (www.raisingdigitalcitizens.com)

INDOOR PLAY

'Dr Peter Gray, one of the world's leading play experts, has defined play
      as follows ...' Gray, Peter. '#2 What Exactly is Play?' petergray.
      substack.com, 25 April 2023.
            (https://petergray.substack.com/p/
      2-what-exactly-is-this-thing-we-call)

'The power of touch releases oxytocin, which improves feelings

of wellbeing and increases trust.' LeWine, H. (reviewer).
'Oxytocin: the love hormone'. health.harvard.edu, 13 June
2023. (https://www.health.harvard.edu/mind-and-mood/
oxytocin-the-love-hormone)

'Play and the common third.' Pedagogy4change. 'The common
third in social pedagogy'. pedagogy4change.org. (https://www.
pedagogy4change.org/the-common-third-in-social-pedagogy/)

'Research shows that we are happier when we win together rather than
winning alone.' Simon-Thomas, Emiliana. 'Do team victories
feel better than individual victories?' greatergood.berkeley.edu, 1
December 2008. (https://greatergood.berkeley.edu/article/item/
do_team_victories_feel_better_than_individual_victories)

See also: Hadi, Jameel, and Johansen, Thure. 'The Common Third: A
kindred spirit to youth work?' sspa-uk.org. (https://sppa-uk.org/
the-common-third/)

' . . . studies show that toddlers play longer, and are more concentrated
and creative, when they have fewer toys.' Dauch, C., Imwalle, M.,
Ocasio, B., and Metz, A. E. 'The influence of the number of toys
in the environment on toddlers' play'. *Infant Behav Dev*. 50:78–87,
February 2018.

'Danes have massage classes in schools because it reduces bullying
and creates more empathy.' Fri for Moberri. 'Børnemassage med
Bamseven – derhjemme' ('Children's massage with Bamseven –
at home'. friformoberri.dk. (https://www.friformobberi.dk/
aktiviteter/boernemassage-med-bamseven%E2%80%AF-
derhjemme/)

See also: Klit, Maria. 'Sadan skabes trygge fællesskaber. Massage
giver færre konflikter' ('This is how safe communities
are created. Massage causes fewer conflicts'). bupl.
dk, 2018. (https://bupl.dk/boern-unge/find-artikler/
saadan-skabes-trygge-faellesskaber-massage-giver-faerre-konflikter)

'What's the difference between pure play and contest play?' Gray,

Peter. '#17 Play, Contest and Games: What are the differences?' petergray.substack.com, 8 August 2023. (https://petergray. substack.com/p/17-play-contest-and-games-what-are)

'Learning how to lose.' Vigsø Grøn, Susanne. 'Lær dit barn at tabe' ('Teach your child to lose'). dr.dk, 22 August 2013. (https://www. dr.dk/levnu/boern/laer-dit-barn-tabe)

See also: Raabæk, Anna. 'Sadan hjælper du den darlige taber' ('How to help the poor loser'). avisen.dk, 17 July 2022. (https://www.avisen. dk/goer-braetspil-til-en-succes-selv-for-den-daarlige-t_661123.aspx)

'The power of *pyt*.' Rosinger, Karen. 'What to do when hygge no longer works'. bbc.com, 18 February 2019. (https://www.bbc.com/travel/ article/20190217-what-to-do-when-hygge-no-longer-works)

SPECIAL DAYS AND RITUALS

'Danes burn more candles than any other country in Europe.' 'Cocoa by candlelight'. economist.com, 29 September 2016. (https://www. economist.com/europe/2016/09/29/cocoa-by-candlelight#_

'Rituals are important because ...' Wendt, Taylor. 'Why family traditions matter'. webmd.com, 6 October 2022. (https://www.webmd.com/ balance/why-family-traditions-matter)

'Forcing children to say thank you isn't so common in Denmark.' Bugge, Mathilde. 'Moderne børneopdragelse beskyldes for at undgå konflikter, men børn har brug for dem' ('Modern child-rearing is accused of avoiding conflict, but children need it'). dr.dk, 14 February 2024. (https://www.dr.dk/nyheder/kultur/ moderne-boerneopdragelse-beskyldes-undgaa-konflikter-men-boern-har-brug-dem)

'The braided Christmas heart is a classic tradition, and you will see them literally everywhere in Denmark.' 'Pleated Christmas hearts'. wikipedia.org. (https://en.wikipedia.org/wiki/ Pleated_Christmas_hearts)

'Discuss and try out the Hygge Oath.' Alexander, Jessica Joelle and
        Sandahl, Iben. *The Danish Way of Parenting: What the Happiest
        People in the World Know about Raising Confident, Capable Kids.*
        TarcherPerigee, 2016.

For some excellent inspiration for spending time with your kids as they get
        older, see: Neufeld, G., and Maté, G. *Hold on to Your Kids: Why parents
        need to matter more than peers.* Vintage Canada, 2004.

BAKING

'Research shows that baking fosters feelings of wellbeing, contributes
        to stress relief and can improve self-esteem and self-confidence.'
        Northern Healthcare. 'The mental health benefits of baking'.
        northernhealthcare.org. (https://www.northernhealthcare.org.uk/
        news-resources/the-mental-health-benefits-of-baking/)

Collier, A. F., and Wayment, H. A. 'Psychological Benefits of the "Maker"
        or Do-It-Yourself Movement in Young Adults: A Pathway Towards
        Subjective Well-Being'. *J Happiness* Stud. 19:1217–1239 (2018).

'A study in the *Journal of Happiness* found that young adults who engage
        in activities like baking experience improved wellbeing in the form
        of better mood repair, social skills and the ability to be present.'
        Conner, Tamlin, Deyoung, Colin and Silvia, Paul. 'Everyday
        creative activity as a path to flourishing'. *Journal of Positive Psychology.*
        13:1–9, 2016.